PINEAL G

Meditation With Hypnosis Method to Open Your
Third Eye

(Activate Your Pineal Gland, Awaken Your Third
Eye & Develop Your Intuition)

William Davis

Published By Zoe Lawson

William Davis

Pineal Gland: Meditation With Hypnosis Method to Open Your Third Eye (Activate Your Pineal Gland, Awaken Your Third Eye & Develop Your Intuition)

ISBN 978-1-77485-266-8

Legal & Disclaimer

The information contained in this book is not designed to replace or take the place of any form of medicine or professional medical advice. The information in this book has been provided for educational and entertainment purposes only.

The information contained in this book has been compiled from sources deemed reliable, and it is accurate to the best of the Author's knowledge; however, the Author cannot guarantee its accuracy and validity and cannot be held liable for any errors or omissions. Changes are periodically made to this book. You must consult your doctor or get professional medical advice before using any of the suggested remedies, techniques, or information in this book.

Upon using the information contained in this book, you agree to hold harmless the Author from and against any damages, costs, and expenses, including any legal fees potentially resulting from the application of any of the information provided by this guide. This disclaimer applies to any damages or injury caused by the use and application, whether directly or indirectly, of any advice or information presented, whether for breach of contract, tort, negligence, personal injury, criminal intent, or under any other cause of action.

You agree to accept all risks of using the information presented inside this book. You need to consult a professional medical practitioner in order to ensure you are both able and healthy enough to participate in this program.

Table of Contents

Introduction

The book I'll guide you through opening the third eye (also known as"the eye of the inside"). It is an esoteric "organ" that is capable of seeing beyond normal sight. It is believed as the main source of insight and understanding. When you've reached its full growth and visions are able to be seen through it will be larger than the ones that are seen through eyes of the physical.

I will go over the various ways to activate your third eye to assist you in achieving spiritual vision. My aim is to help you gain an understanding of perception that is new as well as increase your awareness as well as foresight and awareness, and challenge your perception of reality.

The third eye is a symbol of an elevated state of consciousness which allows for a deeper perception of the world around us and our role within it. Hindus call it the ajna, which literally translates to "perceive". Ajna is sixth chakra of seven or points of contact for subtle energy channels through which vital energy of life flows. They are component of our sub-conscious (non-physical) body that is comprised by the mind, the intelligence and the ego. Energy from the outside gets into our bodies through the chakra of ajna.

Telepathy, clairvoyanceand dream interpretation, and foresight vision are all connected to the ajna Chakra and the ajna Chakra, and all other experiences that go beyond physical sense. Third eye chakra has an extremely deep connection with the spiritual realm. It is in this center that intuition lives and everything that is beyond physical manifestation. When it is active, it creates mental clarity and the ability to "see" beyond the obvious.

The third eye's vision are manifested in a variety of ways. A lot of people believe that this view can reveal supernatural beings or people, places or even places. However, that's not always the situation. Visions can take on various forms dependent on the individual and how well developed your third eye. Although it is possible to have detailed visions and flashes however, the main thing you get from exploring spirituality is self-knowledge. This means knowing your path in life and developing confidence even in the most difficult periods.

If our eyes are fully open we begin to perceive the truth which is reflected within our minds and hearts. This new perspective helps us to let go of our self-centered fantasies that we are constantly living in by letting the abilities that we were able to develop as children come back to us in our adulthood.

The organ that senses the eye's third is called the pineal gland. It is a tiny gland that's endocrine and photosensitive located in the middle of the brain. It produces the hormone melatonin. It is known to regulate the patterns of sleep and wake and is believed to be the originator of dimethyltryptamine, an endogenous hallucinogen to the human body.

The function of the pineal gland was not known until recent and for spiritual schools and cultures across the world, it's been believed to be an instrument that bridges the world of the physical and the spiritual. It is believed to be the primary resource of energy spiritual available to human beings and, in reality the development of psychic capabilities is linked to this organ, believed to be the source of higher-vision, from the beginning of time.

Due to natural evolution the pineal gland was unable to maintain its ability to shield itself from blood brain barrier, and is susceptible to harmful toxic substances that enter the bloodstream. The majority of pineal glands in people are nearly completely calcified at the point of adulthood. The reason for this is because of the harmful substances that are present in the vast majority of the products we make use of, which causes a build-up in calcium phosphate crystals. Luckily, by taking care of your body and detoxification, you can revive your pineal gland and also open the eye of your third.

If you do not maintain that third eye all the benefits and capabilities that I have just mentioned are diminished. The third eye that is closed can be linked to confusion, jealousy insecurity, envy, cynicism anxiety, pessimism, as well as narrow-minded thinking. There is good news you can find solutions for this issue, like a variety of strategies and methods that encourage the stimulation of your pineal gland as well as the opening of the third eye. The ultimate goal is to be able to see the world as it is in the event that it isn't satisfactory or unsubstantial.

We will look at the 10 methods of activation that can assist you in awakening your pineal gland as well as open your third eye, allowing you to connect with your intuition and uncover the truth about you as well as the universe around you. They include:

.Detoxifying you pineal gland: You will discover how to cleanse and decalcify your pineal glandto enhance its capabilities.

The Candle technique A simple visualization technique which will assist you in focusing more of your energy on the chakra of your third eye.

The Veil technique is a method of training the third eye that will show you how to utilize the pineal gland to focus objects even in darkness.

The See technique is a third eye opening technique that can take your eye's third-eye perception to the next level through the aid by guided visualization.

Focus meditation is a simple technique of meditation that can boost the power of your third eye's sense.

Awakening meditation: a satisfying meditation practice designed to work your eye's third and increase you spiritual sight.

Kundalini yoga: You will discover the principles of kundalini yoga, and how you can incorporate this practice to the growth of your third eye.

Take crystals and learn which crystals will enhance the activity of your third eye and help you to awaken your spirituality.

Massage using magnets: You will learn about the amazing influence that electromagnetic fields have on pineal gland's functions and how you can utilize magnets to trigger your third eye.

Technological Aid: You'll be taught about brainwave entrainment as well as how to make use of music to stimulate the pineal gland.

It isn't necessary to have any expertise or knowledge about any of the techniques mentioned above. We recommend that you put aside all you've been reading or heard about to date, so that you can fully immerse yourself in this experience with a fresh perspective.

Keep in mind that only by accepting the reality of things as they are can we determine what's possible to accept it, and then transform it, if that's what we're seeking. Our heart, our consciousness or soul, or our spirit - or whatever we prefer to label it- is the one that shows us the method. However, sometimes we close the door to it and decide to lie to ourselves in fear of what we might find out. We hope that this book helps you to gain access for your voice, and help you find the truth. The third eye can help you see things that your eyesight will never be capable of seeing.

Chapter 1: Introduction To The Third Eye Philosophy

The ancient Hermetic philosophy states that in the Golden Age, our forefathers had the "Third Eye" situated on their foreheads. Through evolution and evolution, this Third Eye gradually transformed into the modern-day pineal gland that is located within the human brain's geometric center. It is the Third Eye organ is not used to perform everyday tasks however it is able to be activated. This awakening is possible through the practice of holistic Yoga and its roots which can be traced back to India. "The third Eye (also known as "trinetra" is depicted with an ear-to-forehead dot.

Hindu mythology is filled with symbols of pinecones. Shiva is One of the most well-known Hindu gods, is always depicted by a pinecone shaped mark on the middle of his forehead which is believed to represent his "Third Eye." The Third Eye or forehead chakra eye is known as Shiva's eye. It is believed to be the repository of all the knowledge of the universe. It is considered that in Hindu mythology that, if it is opened the Third Eye could destroy everything it sees. This makes it an effective symbol of knowledge, which can annihilate ignorance.

It transcends the physical realm since there isn't a single explicit reference to it. It is interesting that the Third Eye is not directly mentioned in the context of the ancient world (though there are numerous indirect references) this supports the possibility that it could be an integral part of daily life that it was able to be understood. Additionally, because communication in ancient times was entirely through the medium that was symbols, it is possible to find lots of symbols that refer towards the Third Eye or at least an energy center that is located between the eyebrows that are closely connected to spiritual awakening as well as soul journeys and self-realization.

The Third Eye transcends physical characteristics to reach it's spiritual meaning. It is believed to be the source of not only all things psychic as well as a place that allows us to be in touch with God, the supreme and higher power. When we are able to master the power of the pineal gland and abilities, we can solve the problem of an organ that is located in the brain, but is not part in the realm of mind. According to the ancient Egyptians the path to freedom can only be gained by breaking away from this contradiction.

Metaphysics is a vast field of study such as the ability to be awake in dreams as well as walking between multiple realities and transcending limitations have its principles firmly enshrined within the Third Eye symbolism. It is considered to be the most fundamental foundational element that is the basis of the entire range of psychic abilities.

The third Eye can be described as an esoteric notion that refers to an invisble eye that can provide vision beyond normal perception. In Hindu spiritual traditions it is known by the name of Anja the energy of chakra. Eastern faiths always acknowledged that the Third Eye as mystic, making it a fundamental element the Indian, Chinese, Buddhist and other Asian traditions. It is believed that the Third Eye philosophy is widely used and practiced in areas where Taoism and Hinduism are flourishing.

It is interesting that New World western cultures have neglected Third Eye symbolism despite pressing evidence in early American art. Examine in depth the Maya, Inca, Aztec and other ancient western civilizations and you'll see how The Third Eye is integral to these cultures. Third Eye depictions are apparent in myths, engravings, and paintings from cultures that go back a number of thousand years.

The idea that Third Eye is a popular concept. Third Eye is widely used in Eastern philosophy, and can be found in many disciplines like Yoga Aikido, aikido, and Qigong. It is located at the heart of Kundalini Yoga, with the well-known chakra system. The Third Eye of the Anja (energy) chakra can be described as the sixth in seven chakras that regulate your body. The chakra is activated or awakened when solar Pingala medium to the right side of the body is in balance in conjunction with lunar Ida ida on the left.

Osiris is the Egyptian god's companions are depicted in two serpents that are entwined as they rise to join in the pine cone. This is an extremely similar depiction of Kundalini energy, or awakening in Hinduism in which serpents are shown ascending in a spiral towards the gland of pineal.

Kundalini Yoga is a specific yoga practice that was not recognized in the Western world for a long time prior to when it was recognized as the current rage that it is now. The yogic doctrine that is the basis of Kundalini Yoga is centered on the awakening of the inner or higher self through stimulating The Third Eye.

Kundalini in Sanskrit translates to enlightenment. This is the Third Eye can grant the person with mystical abilities that are profound, like higher awareness, higher awareness, advanced clairvoyance and a variety of self-healing capabilities. In essence, The Third Eye indicates spiritual enlightenment and gives the practitioner inner insight or a glimpse of the eternal nature of their being.

The sun's design, with the sun on the right and the moon on the left, along with an eye that is located in the middle on the forehead. It was also a common element on a variety of sketches and objects of Freemasons, Western history's oldest Secret Society. Its Third Eye is often depicted as being between the solar masculine energyof Pingala and the lunar feminine energy - ida.

Chapter 2: Reactivating The Third Eye

What's The Third Eye?

We haven't yet answered the question to date. This question is, which is exactly the role of the third eye? The third eye isn't only a bodily organ that is called the pineal gland, however it's also a mythological and esoteric organ. It is usually referred to as an organ with the capacity to see things that are beyond the scope of our senses. Sometimes , this is described as a chakra, specifically when it is used in Hindu Tradition. In the west, the third eye has been symbolized over the centuries through the symbol of the pine cone.

The best way to see the eye of third is like an entrance. The third eye is able to communicate with the consciousness's the inner and outer worlds. It is also able to function like a lung cleanse harmful substances that might try to enter your body. We could also think of the third eye as a functions as a light switch. When it is turned on, it responds to signals that come from higher levels of consciousness. This means that the body functions at a higher energy level. In this way, it's obvious that the Third Eye has many purposes.

The activation of the third eye could be beneficial for the esoteric scholar. What we have observed is that when your third eye starts to lose its calcium and become open, health issues disappear like dust. They include physical and mental issues as also mental and spiritual ones.

The third eye is a function in the sense of being an intermediary to your higher self. Through it that contact with our higher selves, or the super soul can be achieved. This is the reason you can find the stones on the forehead's center in a few Eastern religions.

The pineal gland acts as the organ which represents the third eye. It is a tiny gland that is located inside the brain in the middle of the forehead. In everyday science, it is the major producer of the hormone melatonin. Melatonin is a key ingredient in controlling the sleep and wake cycles of an individual. It is small however it is also shaped as the shape of a pine cone. This is the reason why the early people in the West employed this symbolism of the cone art designs, architecture, and even designs.

The temple was built in the past as an imitation of the human body. This means to say that it was believed that the Third Eye would represent the principal entrance to the body. Remember this symbol when we explore the third eye further. Everything in reality must be viewed as a huge network. In addition, it is comprised of smaller networks as well as larger ones. In a way , it is like the Hologram. Micro is macro. External is what is internal. This is the reason why the ancients constructed temples of the ancient religions around the globe. The third eye of a temple is its entry point. It is the gateway to the spiritual and the everyday.

The First Exercise

The first session is focused on getting the ability to detect the third eye's position between each eyebrow. After the initial practice, you'll be capable of being able to, more or less feel your third eye whenever you'd like to. Once this practice is completed the practice should be followed by another meditation that I will go over further down.

This technique doesn't need any special timing. Also, it doesn't require a dress code or ritual. It's simple and could be a test of absolute the intensity. Like I said don't jump to conclusions. Don't imagine that you have a third eye. Don't imagine your third eye. Instead, you should simply feel the feeling that comes from the eye, which exists within your body. It is precisely this energy that we'll use to expand and unlock in the future.

What to Do? to Do It.

This is best practice in a quiet environment where no one else is present. The space you'll be using will be indoors and peaceful.

You should ensure that you are not distracted by anything that could hinder your focus during this exercise. This is more than the sound. Wearing clothing that is pressing on your body, for instance, must be taken off. This can include things like jewelry , as well as your belt.

Then slowly slide down to the floor, then lay to your side. To avoid being distracted by pain, you must have something that is on the ground. It could be carpet, a mat and even blankets is entirely up to you. Letting your arms fall down behind your. Your palms should be pointed upwards towards the roof. The overall posture is comfortable, and your legs should be to the front.

Let the eyes relax until they're closed. They must remain that way until the conclusion to the workout. You should not do anything for a short period of time. Relax, breathe, and let your mind calm down.

Begin to be conscious to your breath. When you start to feel your diaphragm contract and expand increase your attention to other areas that comprise your body. Feel your feet. Feel the feeling of having hands. Relax your attention when new sensations come up. Be in the flow of flow of the.

Concentrate your attention on your right hand. Feel the the energy contained inside it. Then slowly move your hand to the right side of between both eyebrows. The hand shouldn't in any way contact the skin.

If the hand rests just over the skin Feel the sensation. There should be a tingling sensation coming from this spot. This is because the energy is wrapped up inside the eye's third chakra. This should happen for about a minute.

Relax your palm and rest it on your chest again. Then, focus upon your 3rd eye. When you are "sensing" your eye,, you will feel a tingling sensation. Some describe it as being pulsing, or pressure. However you want to describe it, something must be recognized.

Continue to be alert. Keep it going for no more than 10 minutes. If the intensity that this experience brings becomes excessively fast all you have to do is look up and then you'll end the experience.

Then, try to keep the practice going, but with no any focus. Let yourself be distracted by other thoughts. Be aware of any fascinating events that occur. This could include experiences, emotions, sensations and colors, voices, or other interesting things.

You are now able to take a step back and open your eyes.

It is recommended to practice this each day before starting. It is possible to notice that each session is different in intensity, as well as various kinds of results. If you were feeling weak at first it could be because you've experienced a lack of energy. Take it on the following day. We'd like to boost the number of days with high energy. This is only possible through constant exercise.

More on the Sensations

Sensations will become a normal after the previous exercise , and much more. Let me begin by discussing the kinds of experiences that may occur in the third eye. The first and most evident experience is the sensation of vibrating. It is also typical to see the colors and light. The final common feeling is that of seeing the purple light. Each of these experiences reveals the progress towards deeper perception. This will be discussed further throughout the work.

Vibration is the main term used to describe the sensation that occurs between the eyes. No matter what you call it sensation, tingling, pressure or any other term it is, they all mean the exact same sensation. The fact that there's an experience is crucial because it indicates that the stimulation of the energy body occurring within the eye of third. The physical body is the most etheric layer of the energetic field of the human body. It is thought it is the nearest thing you can get to your physical body. This body has been referred to as Prana in the old Indian religions. Farther East In China it was referred to as Qi. The vibrations are of different levels that range from the most gentle and intense.

Another experience that can occur in this session is the visualisation of various kinds of lights. These typically signify a form of energy field that glows like clouds. When you observe such lights, it is a sign that you've activated beyond the etheric realms and have tapped in to your astral body. The astral body lies between the higher realms of astral reality and the more delicate the etheric body. It's located in the middle which is akin to. Lights are present in the realm of light and beyond, but when you do this exercise , the majority of illumination you feel will come through the body of astral. If you experience this kind of progress, it means that your third eye is in the process of opening.

The final sensation we talked about is the potential for a violet color light or a purple-colored imprint or design. It is common for this color to appear in the light of a purple. isn't experienced in the third eye however it is visible throughout the entire space around the person you are. People who have developed the science behind Third Eye experience in past times have referred to this feeling Astral Space. It is interesting to note that this light is also part the spectrum. It is possible that what appears to be purple can also be seen as blues with darker shades to the most dark black. It is important to be aware of the colors they represent and their relationship with space as this is the real nature of these hues.

Make sure to do the exercise consistently. The purpose of the first Exercise is to move throughout the sub-conscious body until you are able to unlock the doorway to the astral. In a sense, this is a way of creating and creating. Keep in mind that the more you practice , the more quickly results will be brought to realization. It is important to persevere.

It might be beneficial to think of that the eye of third is a type of tunnel. In a sense, it's very similar to an organ which can be switched off and on. But its network is linked to other organs in the body. So, although we'll begin by examining an eye that is a structure in the middle of the eye but we will move beyond this simplified view.

Chapter 3: The Pineal Gland

What's the function that is responsible for the sixth sense? It's the pineal gland. together with the pituitary gland in intense concentration, acting as the third Eye. Many people seek out meditation to improve consciousness of their pineal gland to stimulate it, and attain inner peace and joy. It is true that we can use the same gland to manifest your desires into reality may seem absurd and awe-inspiring yet it's real.

It is known that as behavior patterns change, the brain ceases to use specific nerve channels - - in the form of neuron bundleswhich then "rewires" to create new channels that adapt and allow you to follow new patterns. This is also the case when, for instance, you are suffering from nerve damage and the brain must change the way that neurons are positioned to enable you to fulfill the functions that were lost to the old nerves. It sounds like a nightmare, however it can occur.

Simpler organisms are able to regenerate new external limbs, but it's not possible for us to do so, and the brain develops new nerves to allow you use different organs or limbs to replace them. A good example is losing their hands and learning how to make use of his feet to accomplish the same things that hands perform. From a psychological perspective when you go through therapy to treat an obsessive-compulsive disorder, your brain will alter the way neurons are wired to accept new, non-obsessive compulsive behaviors and the old ones are likely to die.

This shows how adaptable the brain is , and also what things that appear impossible actually aren't. They can be accomplished after the brain has been instructed to perform something that is out of the norm. The organ in play in this case can be the pineal gland. It communicates with the brain, which is essentially a servile servant that is conditioned. If your brain believes it's not able to perform something, because it's what you've been taught throughout your existence, it will follow this instruction. If , however, using the use of hypnosis as an example the brain reversibly alters its own conditioning, either in a temporary or permanent way it is free to do whatever it's instructed to do during that state.

This is one reason why these"miraculous cures" are so popular "miraculous" treatments have been found at Lourdes. Let us state immediately that there isn't an utterly 100 "cure" rates at Lourdes and it is clear it is not possible to find anything there apart from the belief of a person that they will cure you. The brain, however, is an additional thing, and that's the only thing that can help you. Patients who visit Lourdes and believe that the water can cure them, get "cures" But a significant proportion of them return to their original condition in a short period of time after they return to their normal surroundings in which the brain has been trained to feel sick. If you truly believe you have been permanently healed, remain completely cured. If you aren't sure the waters actually work are not cured whatsoever.

What's the problem?

You are. The process of changing the patterns that are conditioned in the brain is possible quickly or gradually. The brain has all the information needed to keep your body in good health. If you're sick, the pattern is interrupted. Through simply entering your mind and instructing it to "cure" this body part, it accesses its database of stored information, reads it and returns it to normal, just similar to a computer that is being fragmented.

The main way to inform the brain what to do is that of the pineal gland. With a variety of techniques, it can be suggested during a hypnotic state (either by yourself or another) as well as a shock remedy such as Lourdes or by a faith healer or simply repeating a consistent message to yourself, establishing an actual hypnotic state informing the brain to restore your body, your brain will be restored to its normal state, which is healthy.

If it isn't able to do so due to a loss of limb, or some other changes, it will try the next best option and reprogram the body to adapt to the loss.

It is not a miracle in it. We didn't know the way that the un-seen sense organ functions, therefore we put it in the hands of God, faith healers, magical, a miracle whatever. The only thing we know regarding any religious element is the necessity for "belief" however, it's conviction that brain is capable of doing it. And with the help of studies conducted by scientists, it can be proven that it can. We already know that the brain is able to heal the body naturally. The issue that hasn't been addressed is that we've reached a point of believing that certain illnesses are incurable, but actually, we have not discovered the solution.

However, all medications require the brain's cooperation to perform the healing. It is possible for the brain to be tricked by a placebo into healing , without actually taking the drug. Insufficient trust has been given to this because drug companies can't earn a lot of money from your health if you don't really need their medicines.

To continue on a direction for a paragraph and a half, one of the main barrier to understanding the real nature of how the brain functions is the idea that money is the only thing. The reality is that the brain is able to manifest everything you require to cure itself without the use of costly drugs. You are able to communicate with your buddies in California without the use of a phone should you desire to master the capability as well as you don't require any other means to shield yourself from harm should you choose to communicate independently via this organ.

BELIEF

The term "Belief" has been used to refer to an underlying belief in God as well as a belief that everything must be granted to an individual by the grace of God. It's also come to mean an apex or creed and has lost its true significance.

The belief system is the key to activating your pineal gland. It's part of the psychic apparatus, or a system that includes your training and the Third Eye and your fundamental belief that you are able to create things for yourself. The problem with what religion is that it takes this natural ability and transforms it into an unobserved power.

You believe God will grant your wishes , then naturally, your wishes will come true for you. However, it is your belief that this is the way it will be that determines it. A lot of people who profess faith in God have a tendency to disprove their faith by putting an obligation on their prayer to God. "They will do it" as well as "If God wants to grant the request, God will" is the main reason for doubting that God will indeed grant the request. If doubts are present then you're not trusting your own abilities to function. You have removed doubt from your beliefs.

A good example could be an example of a Christian Science follower who won't undergo any medical treatment, believing that God for healing and then dying of a illness that isn't happening. This is especially dangerous in the event that parents refuse to allow their children suffering from illness to be treated by a doctor and they die. It shows that people are blindly accepting an orthodox religious view and believing that God to instantly reach out and heal them. It is only possible when the person's faith goes beyond mere prayer and into a more profound mental state that allows healing to happen. Only a few people believe in this either within themselves or in the existence of God.

But it isn't just about healing, too. If you'd like to get money, for instance, but you aren't sure what to do or an avenue where money will be able to reach you, it will not occur. Children typically express their financial needs even in the face of resistance because they must or their children will starve. The need to be a good parent will force the belief system to express your requirements.

In the story of the same name, "Mama's Bank Account," by Kathryn Forbes, this example was clearly illustrated. A mother from the United States with four kids and small means would lie to the children she owned an account with a bank but was hesitant about using it. She would then tell her children to look for ways to earn cash so they didn't have to spend their account. When Miss Forbes published her first novel, she presented the money at the request of her Mama and instructed her to put it in the account. Then, her Mama admitted that there had never been a bank account, but she claimed there was one to ensure children wouldn't be worried and it also helped them come up with ways to raise funds so that the account would not be exhausted.

This is an amazing tale of how it all is put into place. If your mother instructs the children to get out there and earn money, you'll discover ways to do it because your mother's guidance is the most effective thing you can get. Once you have that, you'll be instantly taught how to make money. I had a wealthy uncle whose mother would plant vegetables and load up his wagon and instruct him to go and sell the vegetables and not come back until they were all sold. He would always say he was grateful to her throughout his life since it was his responsibility to figure out how to sell his products without failing and eventually he was rich.

Dr. Wayne Dyer - who is an extremely intelligent genius in creating your own desires to improve yourself He wrote a book called You'll See It Once You Believe In It. The entire book is encapsulated in the title. If you let that single word guide you, then everything else will naturally take care of itself and you'll simply be able to move with your conviction to manifest the positive things you'd like to achieve.

The whole book is based on the notion that you must look into your own thoughts and your emotions to determine whether you believe that you are able to be able to manifest your desires as well as your desires by imagining and transforming them into reality. We all have a tendency to easily manifest our needs since we know that we must do it or go to the pit of despair. A few people don't believe that in themselves at all and are living in the streets.

Certain moral and religious beliefs lead us to believe that we're not deserving of the things we want , and because of some reason Heaven or God doesn't allow our desires because we're sinful, or unworthy. In the end, we find the Government is distributing millions of dollars for naughty people who are using the money for golf excursions, and we ask what the reason is that God "allows" it , when children live within motel accommodations. The reason is that the lack of morality lets people indulge in total bliss without concern for any other person, whereas the masses who are suffering in a sense think they require the support of a government as they are unable to accomplish it by themselves. However, there are those who know how to make use of the system for those who are poor to help them, just as billionaires utilize it at the top level. The whole system is based on the conviction that the welfare recipients who believe that the government ought to take care of them due to the fact that they are poor. The rich cats that are apex predators of every free cash they can find, regardless of regardless of whether or not it hurts the government that provides them with the money.

People who think they must pay their bills but struggle and get into financial trouble because they believe they have morality about their debts, and are honest. They also pay their debts and thrive and are content with their overall moral well-being.

It's not about what you believe - it's the actuality of your belief that is shown.

In relation to the goal in this text, the mechanism that we will use here is that you've got an established set of beliefs that you have accumulated through you or others, which tells your Third Eye what it should manifest. If you believe that you must manifest love, money, sexuality or something else you believe in, you Third

Eye will give you what your beliefs and system of belief tells it to. If you don't believe that you are able to manifest love, money, or anything else, you're Third Eye will show the feeling of loneliness, poverty, or even misery in the way you think it should.

It's that simple. It would be tedious.

Add this to the list: belief is a psychic tool in your mind that stimulates the pineal gland, telling it what you want to manifest. It's the operating device or system. It is the one that makes things happen.

Chapter 4: Technique Of Clearing Your Mind

There is a small amount of energy on the Third Eye forehead region. This technique is designed to bring this vibration into you, so that you are able to develop it. The technique is intended to be used only once in order to get the Third Eye. Then, you can keep practicing other techniques of meditation.

The first step is to choose a suitable day for this. Pick a day that is low stress and minimal to no anxiety. It is recommended to begin the day just in the middle of a full moon If you can. It is always best to select a location that is suitable. It is important to find a peaceful location with no disturbances or distractions. It is possible to do this by yourself or with a companion or in the group. The experience is more intense when you are in a group.

Before you begin the process, it is important to understand that this isn't any kind of meditation method whatsoever. It's not a form of an exercise in visualization. It's a method that lets you rid your mind of everything. The aim is to fully relax, completely rid your mind of all thoughts, and open your heart up to the possibility of being fully filled. You should not be imagining nor visualization or thinking. Let the experience unfold before you.

For this exercise place your body to the ground flat. Set your hands by your sides, stretching across the sides of your body. Keep your palms raised. Legs should remain straight with your eyes closed.

Relax. Utilize a breathing method. Keep your attention upon your breath for a few minutes.

You should now begin the throat with a vibration. (You can practice this prior to.) Allow your breath to roll over your vocal

43

box and create an ebb. It should be quiet and soft. It's not about the sound. It's all about the vibration. When air is circulating across your microphone and you feel the vibration due to friction and you will hear a low humming. Don't be concerned if it's precisely right. Continue to do it for several minutes (for as long as 10 minutes).

The goal should be to "be alert" and not think about or imagining. Be conscious. Let your mind wander. Let it flow freely. Allow any energy that you feel move through you. If you notice a sensation or a sensation within your body, don't put it off or think about it. Simply let it occur.

After about 10 minutes of this, lift the other hand above your face. While your palm is in front of you, place the palm's center directly over your forehead and then place it at a point in between the eyes. Don't touch any part on your face. Keep your hands near your face but without touching it. Keep your hand in this position. Maintain your breathing. Keep your eyes shut. Keep your throat moving. Be conscious of the Third Eye forehead.

After about 10 minutes after a while, lower your hands back on the floor. Continue to vibrate your throat.

It is possible to feel an itch between your eyes or inside your forehead. You may feel the sensation of a buzzing or tingling or a vibrating. It might feel like feeling of pressure or weight inside your head.

Make sure your mind is clear. Let it unfold. Close your eyes.

When you are aware of your forehead's vibration, link it to your throat vibrating mentally. Pay attention to both frequencies and feel them merging as one.

If you are experiencing sensations elsewhere in your body, do not pay attention to these sensations. Allow them to happen. This is the normal process.

This process should continue for approximately ten minutes. Do not think or visualisations or meditations. Maintain a calm mind. Relax and enjoy the journey.

Stop the throat vibrations. Relax and remain still. Close your eyes. Don't try to notice anything, not even the slightest vibration. Only be aware of the Third Eye region on your forehead. Repeat this process for approximately 10 minutes.

If you experience or feel lights, colors, or energy in your eyes, or on your head or forehead This is the third Eye activating.

Chapter 5: Mindfulness Meditation - Higher Levels Of Consciousness

The more energy that is released flows, the more spiritual boost that the meditator receives. The fire-like sparks that emanate through the mouth of kundalini snake enter the brain's hemispheres stimulating them more to active activity. The meditator is able to experience the most profound ecstasy, peace, and joy. It is as if the entire body is swept away into the ocean of bliss and happiness.

Through stimulation of the right hemisphere, the hidden potentialities of perception beyond the physical such as clairvoyanceand the clairaudience, telepathy and many more are brought to the forefront. The consciousness begins to expand and expand beyond its limits by opening to possibilities for cosmic unity that are new. Self-identity is beginning to leap into the ever-expanding space of the mind of the universe. This level of understanding of space and time is a reward for the adept for all of his efforts.

Here are some guided meditations to help you reach greater levels of consciousness and manage your internal energy.

A meditation on Clouds of Light

Find a comfy spot to take a break and relax. Relax and let your thoughts freely flow as you move, come and go as you're only an observer. Take a deep breathand keep your breath. Examine for tension in your body. If you spot areas of tension you should release them. Do this when you exhale, remove anything that stops you from relaxed. Breathe deeply again. When you exhale, let go of all energy and thoughts from your body. Take a deep breath. Feel a new energy coming into the body. Breathe in new possibilities , and let the body feel more light. Relax and relax more until you are no longer feeling your body.

If you are relaxed, think of an ethereal mist that vibrates around you. Lightness allows you to effortlessly pass through this fog but your body has an edgier density. The energy clouds slowly move around your. Take a seat on one Feel secure. The cloud lifts your spirits and transports you to a vast universe. The lines between space and time disappear. You are in the world of endless beauty and infinite possibilities. You're floating in the cloud and feel the lightness you've become. You suddenly see a huge rock beneath; the cloud gently falls and then effortlessly upon an unintentionally shaped rock.

Feel the power of the rock Feel the strength radiating from the stone. As you look back you see a huge river. It is difficult to determine the point at which it starts and where it will end. You are amazed by the stream of water. It's an endless stream of energy that is a life-giving river. It is a pleasure to walk close to it and attempt to study its hue as well as experience it with all your being. What sounds are you hearing? The light is shining for you, therefore you are safe to enter the water, walk across it, and scurry along the streamand, at any time you'd like to you to stop, do so.

Relax and focus on the things you require most right now. What is your goal? What are the emotions that will accompany you in the path to your desired goal? Be aware of the energies associated with these feelings and feel how it flows through your body's light and burns, pulses. Inhale the energy of your entire being. Try to look at the paintings of images, images, or symbols that are connected to it. They will appear in front of your eye's own and you will be able to focus on them.

If you're completely flooded with this energy, go into the river, melt for a few seconds in it and purify the energy before releasing it back into the water. Notice how the energy cloud forms out of your body, is absorbed by the waters, then then slowly disappears into the river. Take a deep breath. Your desires merge with the source of your life. Relax in the flow of life for a while. Take a deep breath and then exit the river. You will notice that the cloud of color covers you once more and you rise along with it. You fall into the cloud, and then return. With each breath you come back to the outside world , and experience peace and happiness.

Sacred Space Meditation

Relax, sit in a comfortable position. Close your eyes, calm your mind. Breathe slowly and deeply. Breathing is a diaphragm. Take a moment to breathe deeply and focus on the spine. It's a pillar that connects heaven and earth.

Feel the energy that is concentrated on the two the ends of the pillar. Let the energy of earth ascend, leave the top on the top of our heads, then then disperse to the Universe. Along with the flow of energy any negative feelings such as anxiety, pain, tension, and tension go away.

Your entire being is full of peace. Let your mind become like the ocean and thoughts appear as bubbles at the surface of the ocean. It is possible to remember your thoughts more easily however for the moment just be a passive observer. Take a deep breath, and slowly slowing your breathing. As you breathe, ease your mind and body and more.

Feel the cool, red fog that is engulfing your. It's not cold, it's not hot You can only feel it through your skin.

You can feel like you're sitting on a cloud, that is firm enough to keep you in place, but extremely cozy and comfy. Every part of your body is supported by a cloud: your legs, arms and back, neck and head, and the entire body feels relaxed. The cloud begins to fall gradually into the red cloud and you are swept away by it. It is very slow to sink; you sink deeper before relaxing even more. The fog starts to change color: from bright red to orange-red.

Gradually, the color transforms into yellow-lemon. Your body is also painted with a the lemon hue. You're floating in a cloud that transports you to the green lawn of summer. You can hear the breeze swaying the grass and feel the blue light that is flowing from the sky.

The light of blue turns to purple and then a moonless night with a dark, peaceful and peaceful. The cloud that you were floating on softly lands.

The fog disperses. You lay on your back, laying on the grass. You feel gentle breezes from the wind. You hear the whispers of insects at night.

No matter where you are wherever you are, there's always something that draws your attention towards you. It could be something such as a person, a feeling, or even an image. The thing you're contemplating could appear close to you as you're in a sacred area of fulfillment of dreams. The world can change and any change can only be made upon your demand. This is your home, and you have and you lived there. Get up, and explore the sacred space you are. You may meet someone you (or in relation to someone else) you've long wished for.

After a time it will be apparent that it is time to depart from the holy place. Be sad about the things you have seen, and leave without regret because you are able to return anytime you like.

Relax on your back and be surrounded by fog. It's dark, as if it were the moonless night sky. You can feel the cloud once more under your arms, feet the neck, back and the head. It supports you and gradually begins to rise.

Relax and watch the gradual shift in colors The dark hue of the sky changes in to shades of blue, cyan yellow, green. Through all this you rise slowly. Yellow turns red, then summer orange. Allow your mind to float as your body begins to slowly return to the physical world. You start getting the feel of the floor beneath your back and realize that you are in the same room as you are. You're returning.

Understanding the benefits of a solid Meditation Practice

It is quickly growing in popularity across all over the Western world. While before, meditation was exclusively practiced by those who were enthused by various spiritual practices, today it is the most common thing to do. Today, in Europe as well as here in the USA the expression "I do meditation" does not trigger an uneasy attitude as previously. What's the purpose? What are the advantages of meditation or mindfulness? Why are so many people practicing it? I'll attempt find the answers in this section. However, let's do the chapter in sequence.

What is meditation?

In 2007, a study published which experimentally proved the hypothesis that was previously known to be true. people have two distinct kinds of self-consciousness. various brain regions are responsible for these. These two kinds of self-awareness can be described as"the narrative modus operandi (story mode self-reference, also known as the narrative mode) as well as the experiential mode (empirical mode and experience mode of self-reference).

Narrative mode can be described as a way that allows us to contemplate our past, current and the future. Its fundamental principle lies in the fact that attention can be either partially or totally absorbed by the thoughts that assign an explanation to what's happening. This is the one responsible for our perception of the person we are as well as what is going on around us, the goals we're trying to achieve as well as what connects us to other people and more. The story mode integrates the present, past, and the future for us to form a single, coherent image.

The empirical mode refers to the ability to see the present moment, and the things that are happening in our current second. Our experience direct consists of a variety of elements. First, the sensations experienced by the aid of our senses (hearing and sight, feeling scent, taste, balance). Additionally, they are inner sensations, such as thoughts, feelings, imagination and inner states.

Meditation is a method of training concentration. When we meditate, we learn to be focused on what we are currently experiencing. We learn to remain fully present to the moment.

Why do we need each of these forms of self-awareness?

Self-awareness is both a form of awareness and vital. Narrative mode helps you perform any act. To perform a task requires you to make the decision. In order to take a choice it is necessary to be able to explain to yourself exactly what is taking place. The medical profession has seen instances of brain damage. of the brain involved in the story process. When this area totally ceases to function one becomes an animal. He doesn't do anything and does not speak.

One time I read about a incident in which an individual was thrown into the water and was drowned. He didn't have a reason to take any action to save himself. In order to have a motive for the event to be a success to be a motive, it is necessary to provide the event with a meaning. If the narrative method is not working, then the event seems meaningless.

The empirical state allows us to live present and be aware of the present moment and what's happening to us. Alongside being able to experience total satisfaction from all pleasant sensations (for instance food, pleasure from eating, listening to music, sex and so on.) We are also more aware of what's going on in the world around us. This means that we are able to define the meaning of the event more precisely. The empiric mode lets us modify the way we describe the events by incorporating what's happening right now.

If the empirical process is not well-trained, our thinking is focused on our beliefs about our own lives and the world, and, in a lesser amount depending on what's happening right now.

Let's take a look at an example:

Victor is a sales representative. He is new to the business. He has attended various trainings at which it was explained the theories. However, he's not great in putting this theory into application. When he talks to the client, typically at certain points the client starts to stop talking, and then the conversation ceases. Victor started to do meditation. He now notices that the contact is gone as he starts to feel enthusiasm and a desire to conclude the deal in the shortest time possible. Gradually, he came to sense this sensation in the beginning and began to behave in a calm manner, despite the exuberance. As time passed, he observed that he felt more at ease.

In this case the practice of meditation can help Victor to be aware of his emotions when having the conversation with a client. This resulted in the realization that he realized the reason for the lack of interaction with the customer. In the end as time passed it was possible to alter his behavior and later, his emotional responses were able to be apprehensive.

Awareness is a feedback mechanism that lets you alter your the way you behave. In the absence of realizing what we feel our actions are usually as if we are on autopilot.

Another illustration:

Andrew is a person who has a tendency to be conflicted according to his personality. When he became angry, the conflict would not let him stop. The war broke out according to a well-known scenario. However, Andrew didn't think about the conflict. Every time he came up with conclusions for himself, and then lived with them. The conclusions usually boiled down to the notion that the opposite side was to blame.

As Andrew began to meditate in the beginning it made him recognize that he was acting aggressively. He also noticed that, often when a dispute arises the person doesn't respond to the root of the matter and instead, he reacts to the manner of how the opposing party responds. This made him react more rationally. Andrew discovered that, from time to time the man would speak stingy and offensive words, the goal for which was offence someone else. He was able to stop at the right time. Mindfulness training helps Andrew more often and more quickly to turn off the autopilot when there is the event of a conflict. He can then take steps to find a peaceful solution to the conflict.

What additional benefits can meditation Offer?

The truth lies in the fact that these mechanisms that control concentration are among the simplest functions in our conscious. Therefore, practicing meditation can affect every aspect in our daily lives. Research-proven and well-studied effects include:

- An increase in attention span. Eliminating the amount of distractions.

Enhancing self-control.

- Increase the threshold for pain.

Enhancing the process of learning as well as memorization.

- Relieves stress and irritation.

Meditation to Find Your Higher Self

As you've seen in the meditation guides The most popular method of meditation is to focus on breathing. Although it's beneficial for enhancing concentration as regards consciousness of your inner self it is necessary to step it up a level. In this regard, I recommend using a method called marking or mental note taking.

Marking is a method that falls under the attention category that does not require any choice. Also we're not looking to pay attention to any particular thing, but instead focus on what is taking place around us. Whatever it is. If we notice something the sensation, we label it with the same word. Maybe we experience certain sensations within our bodies. Maybe we're contemplating something. Perhaps we are looking for something. Perhaps we think of something. Anything. In one word.

There are a variety of marking options that are not a decision. It is possible to start with any of them. It is best to only use three words: feel, see, hear and feel. Additionally, each word may be used to describe both external sensations as well as internal. For instance, the term "hear" can refer to the perception of the auditory organs as well as the notion that "sounds" within the head.

When it comes to the best time to meditation, 10 minutes a day is sufficient to begin. It is best to pick the time of day when nobody would bother you.

When you meditate, you may be lying, sitting, standing or walk. Eyes can be closed or open. You can also sit in a chair or on the floor. This isn't all that crucial initially. It is crucial to keep in mind that meditation is a long-term game. Therefore, at the beginning it is best not to go overboard.

Meditation is often associated connected to Buddhist monasteries, where the people seek to be enlightened. But it is a fact that enlightenment is not considered a serious concept, and instead is often used to refer to an impossible goal that one would be striving for for the rest of their life time.

Perhaps, by bringing up this subject may be a bit odd to some, however, you should take the chance. The process of awakening is a real and very significant shift in the functioning of the human mind that could occur due to your practice of mindfulness. It has was my experience. It occurs suddenly in one moment. It is described in Buddhist texts, you will find descriptions of various stages of awakening. Each of these stages will lead to a dramatic improvement in the fundamental awareness level.

It isn't an easy feat. However, it's not impossible. As per Daniel Ingram, whose book helped me understand the technical aspects of meditation, it's much easier than completing a degree at an institution of higher learning. In addition it's not necessary to reside in the monastery. If you practice meditation for at least an hour per day and get recommendations from a seasoned instructor, I would say it could take anywhere from a few months to a few years with no interruption to your normal life. If you're interested in it seek out such an instructor.

Meditation has an enormously positive effect on my daily life. I am convinced that the more you progress and the more you be able to comprehend what I am talking about. Have fun!

Chapter 6: What Meditation Can Help You Awaken Your Third Eye

The concept of being able awaken the eye's third is founded on the idea that the pineal gland is sort of dormant. by a small amount of stimulation is enough to activate the gland. In order to stimulate the eye's third, you'll begin to become conscious of things that your senses naturally aren't capable of seeing. There are many advantages to opening the third eye, however it can take time and you need to be open to the concept. Let's look at some things you can try to open your third eye.

Third eye and meditation

To open your third eye and begin working on your higher state of consciousness, it is essential for the pituitary gland as well as the pineal gland cooperate. This will require controlled mindfulness and relaxation techniques. When the proper relationship is created inside your body when you are using the pineal gland a kind of magnetic field will be generated. The negative and positive energy will be connected and result in a strength of the force, resulting in an effect of "light within your head".

The first thing you could think about doing is a little meditation. A lot of people prefer to practice the form of meditation that helps you focus your energy. In this practice you should concentrate your attention on the midpoint in between the pituitary gland as well as your pineal gland. By doing this, you'll be able to create an electric field around the pineal gland. Your creative mind will begin to imagine different things, and your brain will generate thoughts that provide an orientation and life to the images you see.

The eye of the third is usually called an organ or light body or energy body and, once it's open, it is able to gain access to the soul's dimensions. When we talk about the soul here, we're thinking of memories of light and energy that reside within the body. These memories are fascinating because they contain current, future and past dimensions of time , or us. It is possible to make use of this light to go through a portal into another dimension, or to go through images and fantasies.

Meditation and the ability to let your third eye open goes hand in hand. In the beginning, you must be able to identify the chakra of that third eye. Keep in mind that these chakras are energy centers of the body which are comprised of seven which align starting from your stomach region until at the very top of your head. Each chakra will take care of the different aspects of your mental, spiritual well-being, as well as physical. It is possible to use meditation to focus on different chakras, but we'll concentrate on the third eye chakra.

You'll be able to spot the third eye chakra at the top of the brain. In essence, it's going to be situated between your eyes, right towards the bridge of the nose. When you meditate and meditating, you should be able to focus your thoughts to this particular chakra for as long as you can. This is the chakra which is responsible for being able to see the world with greater clarity and can allow you connect with your surroundings in ways you've never imagined But first, you must focus on the proper location.

When you're focused on your third eye you must ensure that you are in the proper environment. It is important to eliminate distractions as much as feasible to ensure you are able to concentrate your third eye to the maximum amount of focus instead of focusing on other things. There are several places you can go that can help you achieve this.

For instance, some think they feel more relaxed when they're in the natural environment. It is possible to meditate outside in case this is most suitable for you to try out. you must choose an area that's likely to be at the ideal temperature and also where you can be completely alone during your meditation, however. There are some who may not be comfortable outdoors or it might be cold and wintery to meditate outdoors. It is okay to meditate indoors. practice with. It is still necessary to locate a space in which you are able to be by yourself in your own home, maybe in a meditation space. Include anything that can allow you to feel at ease like an ottoman to rest on, candles and some soothing music.

The second aspect you should focus on is your posture. The connection between your body and mind is crucial while you work in meditation. The more relaxed you feel in your surroundings, the more easy you will find it easier to concentrate on your third eye. The most comfortable posture to work with is sitting across the floor. If you're not used being seated on the floor, try the process slowly, to allow your body to feel comfortable. Some people prefer working using a cushion, so that they feel more at ease sitting on the floor as well.

If you are finding that it's uncomfortable to sit down for a while it's fine. Some people are inclined to practice what's called walking meditation. The rhythmic sound of your footsteps are comforting also. Take your time when doing this, and ensure that your path is free of obstructions so that you don't have to think about where you're taking you during this time.

Once you're on the ground and feeling comfortable now is the time to meditate with a specific object. This can be a physical object or thought you are able to focus on so that your mind isn't tempted to wander away too much. Candles are a very popular option however, you are able to choose any other option you'd like. Others prefer the soothing mantra that will keep them focused and ensure they don't wander off in their thoughts.

The most important thing to remember here is to make the meditation part of your daily routine. The third eye's awakening isn't something you can do only one time and assume that everything will be perfect forever. You must keep working in the right direction, striving to build it up and stay awake. A 15 minute session of meditation could make all the difference in your day, and you won't need to devote a lot of time doing it.

There are many different kinds of meditation you could try. Many people prefer sticking with the one we discussed earlier. Sometimes, simply being silence and taking a few deep breaths can bring about a change also. If you're not able to keep your mind clear and peaceful at this point (this isn't easy when you are engaged in all of the things that stress you out or taking place within your daily life) there are some other options that you could test.

For example, doing visualization exercises can help out. It's similar to the one we discussed earlier with the cloud moving through your body, releasing the tension. It provides you something else to focus on and make you feel better. The addition of some sound can be able to make a huge change in the way your mind can focus on the positive things.

Meditation is typically the most effective option for opening your third eye. It's simple but there are options to test, and it's something everyone should try. Begin to practice mindfulness every day, and putting an element of thought to the third eye. You will be able open the third eye quickly.

Make yourself more aware

Another strategy you can employ is to be conscious. What that means is that you'll be more conscious of what's happening within you. You will pay more attention to the physical sensations you experience and your mood. It will help you not only become more aware to your actions but also the entire world surrounding you. As you become more aware, you must realize that this isn't an opportunity to be judgmental. It is your job to look around and observe what's happening and without making a judgment about whether or not it's correct or not.

Get outside and enjoy nature. An effective method to begin to master the practice of being mindful is to go outdoors and spend more time in the natural world. Being mindful is beneficial to your eye's third as it actually helps you become more conscious of it. You don't need to do something crazy, but going for a walk every day will benefit you. Our modern world is immersed in technology all every minute having some time to relax and get out in the natural world can make a significant impact.

Creative thinking will be the following thing you could be focused on. We are so distracted by work and school and all the other tasks we need to accomplish each day that we don't spend the time to think creatively. There are many ways to be creative , and when we choose to do so, we're allowing us to be authentic to the person we are. You could choose to draw, paint or take photos or write, study, and even to create or play music. It's all yours to decide.

Being conscious means you will be focusing on the little things. It's easy to become overwhelmed by the daily routine. Making the effort to become more attentive can help us relax and also utilize the third eye. Paying attention to a few minor details of our day-to-day routines can be beneficial.

The benefits of the third eye

The practice of mindfulness and meditation can do great things in opening up the third eye. A lot of people overlook the third eye, allowing it to shut and rarely used. They might not be aware of the damage they are doing to themselves, and to others by doing this. There are many reasons and advantages to why you should get your third eye open and with just a time and effort you can get it done.

The primary benefit you'll see is that it helps you be more relaxed. Once you've learned to open your third eye, you'll begin to reap the wonderful benefits associated with it. Actually there are lots of people who believe that once they have opened the eye of their third, they be more peaceful. This could be because they can have a more positive feeling of self-compassion through the process. Furthermore, as you're being more mindful of your own self as a person, you are more likely to be self-loving.

Another advantage is that you'll have greater wisdom. A lot of people wish to to unlock the third eye since it will give them more insight. As you can make use of the third eye to enhance your awareness about the environment around you you're more likely to make better choices and be able to comprehend the people who surround you and be more knowledgeable all around. Additionally, you can use this to better understand your own self as well.

In the end, opening your third eye could help you improve your physical well-being. The third eye opening can aid in reducing the stress levels in your life and make you more aware and calm. There are numerous physical benefits of decreasing stress levels for example, reducing the issues with depression as well as reducing the high pressure. You may even notice healthier looking skin, less headaches and stomach upsets during the process.

The process of opening your third eye may require some time to complete. It's not something you'll achieve over night. If you're committed to the process and incorporating some mindfulness and meditation into your everyday life you will be able to notice a huge difference. it won't be long for you to begin to experience the benefits we've discussed in terms of awakening your third eye.

Chapter 7: Making Use Of The Third Eye

As we've seen in our previous chapters, the advantages from opening your Third Eye are many ranging from increased intuition, enhanced imagination, and enhanced memory, to greater psychic abilities. Connecting with the spiritual world is among the most beneficial uses to make use of your Third Eye. If the Third Eye is open it is able to communicate with the spiritual realm constantly. You will notice increased intuition (you will get additional information coming from the spirit realm). In time, you will discover how to effectively communicate with the spiritual realm.

People who have had body experiences claim they observed a silver cord which connected their third eye to their astral bodies. It is likely that your spiritual world is determined by how you utilize the Third Eye. Close your eyes physically to give yourself the chance to utilize the incredible powers that the pineal gland has. You can control your breathing in similarly to how you breathe during meditation. Concentrate upon your 3rd eye, to be able to perceive tunnels and colors. Close your eyes and visualize the things you want to feel. Your intuition will guide your actions. As you continue to training, you'll be able to become proficient in the process. It is possible to see auras around things and people, and other entities (not necessarily ghosts and elementals) dependent on your proficiency using the third eye.

Other experiences of opening the Third Eye

When you open your third eye you'll be experiencing strange sensations that could include:

1. Tingling sensation or pressure. This can be felt in the area between the eyebrows. It occurs when you are picking the

energetic signals, or when the chakras are awakening.

2. Connectivity with Spirit. It is possible to feel the realm of spirit. You can have guides from the spirit world as well as angels, as well as your loved ones who are in heaven.

3. The desire to stay away from negativity. You'll start to be more emotional towards others because you're influencing their feelings and emotions. Soon, you'll realize you're extremely negative or dramatic.

4. The desire to eat Healthier Foods. You'll start to stay away from junk food and will have the desire for foods that are vibrational like fruits and vegetables to maintain your health and happiness.

5. The desire to study and become more spiritual. You'll want to learn and read while you travel the path of spirituality.

6. Vivid Dreams. The waking of the mind triggers people to dream more frequently due to:

* While you sleep you will not feel any resistance.

* You're in a position to reach other consciousness levels, such as dreams. Keep a journal of your experiences.

7. A heightened sensitivity of your physical Sensors. Your hearing will increase You will notice flashes of light in the corner of your eyes. This is when your senses of perception are getting more powerful.

8. Intuition. It is possible to start getting the sensation that something will occur. For some people, this is thrilling but to some it can be very scary. To keep from being scared be sure that you will not be a victim of frightening visions. Also, you should practice how to utilize the psychic powers until you are at ease.

9. Headaches. They are typical during the wake-up process due to the energy surge. Warm your feet with warm water, mixed in essential oils, or Epsom salt. This will redirect the focus of your head towards

your feet. It is also possible to seek medical attention from your physician.

10. Losing Friends - As a result of awakening your third eye, you'll begin to perceive people and objects differently. Your family and friends who surround you will perceive you in a different way. After a while you'll lose some of your friends , and the universe is fair, as you'll be able to meet more people to join your life.

Chapter 8: Learning To Activate The Third Eye

The ability to activate the third eye is the first step to experiencing higher, multi-dimensional levels of consciousness. It is vital to ensure that while you're learning to improve your psychic abilities it is a good idea to spend some time learning about your shadow vision and fears , as they are what is blocking your intuition. It will block the flow of information that is being able to flow through you. Your fears, a good color, can hinder your feelings.

There's a chance for mistranslation between the truth about what the universe is to you as well as what you eventually see based on your own perspective within the overall perspectivethat you have, which you name God. This means that you'll be communicating by focusing on your own perspective. And the more conscious you become about yourself, particularly of your fears and fears, the less likely you'll be to make a mistake or interpret it according to your own beliefs. believing.

Eat an oriented diet

The first step to open the third eye chakra. This is done by consume a diet that is spiritually focused and eat a vegan or a raw food diet. Foods that are grounded will allow you to enter a higher real world than those that aren't grounded, which allows the expansion of your awareness to a higher level. Beware of water with fluoride as it will affect the pineal gland.

Certain foods that you could add to your diet if you're looking to open the third eye chakra are the raw cacao plant, chakra mushrooms juice from apple cider vinegar in raw form, lemons blueberries, goji berries the pawpaw, lavender mangoes the grapefruit juice Spirulina, blue, and green algae, iodine Zeolite Jason, bentonite clay chlorophyll, cilantro honey, coconut oil seaweed, hemp seeds as well as noni juice.

Get rid of your physical visions

If you wish to to activate the chakra, you need to stop seeing through your eyes when you are trying to open your third. The way to do this is you must either shut your eyes or locate an area of complete darkness that is completely free of electronic screens or any other source of light.

In an area that is dark the pineal gland that is the expression that is the third eye is stimulated to produce Melatonin. Melatonin plays an extremely significant part in allowing your brain to enter an experience where you feel a higher level of consciousness, which isn't restricted to the 3rd dimension. Melatonin is the reason why it is an essential component of sleep as it is an out-of-body experience.

Exercise in meditation to open the third eye chakra

For the first time, you can sit with your arms above your head, or lie down and watch your breath. Your breath is the gateway between different dimensions, and the third dimension that connects the various levels of conscious. Thus, you take note of your breath out and in and breathe out through your nose. Then attempt to breathe through your mouth. Then, you watch your thoughts and not try to resist the thought; because when you are unable to try to avoid this idea, you will be focusing on the thought and in the process the thought comes back.

You just watch your thoughts as they pop up and let them move on. You can read your thoughts , and then attempt to pay attention and focus around your neck, face along with behind your ears. When you do this, you'll notice the amount of energy on your face and specifically, what the tension could cause a problem with regards to the energy flow from one place to another way for to allow the Third Eye to open. Focus on your paying attention, and then try to relax your muscles in your face, ears, and all other places that your scalp is located, pay concentration.

The second part

In the next step attempt to breathe deep throughout and hold breath as long as you can. You should then make a small space between your jaw's bottom and your top jaw, just enough to allow your tongue to be able to fit between your teeth. When you exhale, you should try to make an exact sound. Your pineal gland is sensitive to sound and therefore, you can use the tone to activate the third eye. When you do this, you have to introduce it to your brain, you must remain in several minutes. The next thing you need to accomplish is to make the sound that sounds like it sounds like thhhhhhhh .....

Make sure to keep your tongue place between your teeth over a lengthy period of time to allow it to be vibrating between your teeth when you exhale. Try to alter the tone and pitch of your breath until you can be able to find something that energizes your body. Try doing this 6 times in a row but be aware that this workout can trigger headaches as you attempt to stimulate a part of your brain that isn't being utilized. This is why you may suffer from headaches and detox symptoms, as well as dizziness, or even start hearing sounds within your head, such as crackling and popping. If this occurs, it's completely normal.

If it isn't a problem for you take it off and move on to the next stage in the workout.

Then, attempt to inhale deeply and keep your breath in for 6 seconds. This is why you should repeat it three times. Then, breathe completely out and breathe deeply and this time, create a different sound which will stimulate your third eye to a greater extent.

The next tone will be May. However, it must sound mayyyyyy. Everyone is affected by various tones, so if you're using the word may it is possible to hear the sound when you begin to buzz the Third Eye Chakra.

When you're singing the tune, be able to feel the vibration in your head that is the third eye region. Whatever sound you hear within that area, attempt to keep it in your mind for this practice and repeat the note 6 times for an entire long, slow breath.

When you hold the tone you may feel sensations of buzzing that are removed from your body, deep into the middle of your brain. It can also extend towards the crown the top of your head. If this happens, you must know that it is completely normal. It is a sign that you are activating your third eye to that you sense the channel. It is an organic channel that is sending sensory signals from physical energy field to the third eye.

Pay attention to your third eye.

This exercise is designed to help you to listen to Your Third Eye. This means that you can do this with your eyes closed in the third it is possible to do this according to your own preference. You can also choose not to perform this exercise, or simply skip it.

With you eyes closed think of that your third eye is closed exactly like the way you shut your eyes in real life. Imagine your third eye opening like you wake up from a deep sleep. If you're having trouble getting it to happen, you may have to put your hands over your Third eye and remain it there. Even if your eyes shut should be able to move your eyes back behind your eyelid in a straight line to look at your third eye.

It is possible that you think that you are eye straining however this exercise can help you to to let your third eye open and engage it. After you've completed it, take a look at the things you see. When you see and what you feel as if you are experiencing sensations. In the beginning, these images could be blurry or you may only see patterns, colors or even outlines. The images at first appear blurry and unclear. Therefore, try to notice the images without making any judgments about it.

When you were born into the physical world, all things seemed blurry and unrecognizable to you. So you'll experience the same phenomenon which will occur when trying to tune into your third eye. Everything may appear blurry at first however, as time passes you'll begin to observe the extra-dimensional world as you view the physical realm. If you are at ease and ready to return to the third dimension take a moment to concentrate on your breath and your entrance to the third dimension. Then, close your eyes and make sure to record exactly what impressions you got.

Do this each day for three consecutive weeks. After you've completed the exercise, you can open your eyes and are begin to observe and observe things that have an more than you can imagine, you'll be able to discern the affirmative assertions clearly.

The affirmative assertion will inform that the reality of dimensionality is intended to be organized in order for you to be able to comprehend it, translate it, and grasp what you're experiencing. It is essential to comprehend that you are in contact with the fourth dimension when you activate your third eye.

The fourth-dimensional reality is instantaneous this means you don't get a cushion of when you activate your 3rd eye. It's not as physical, in which you are able to imagine a concept and wait many hours before it can appear, and yet it will not appear. After doing this several times, you are able to begin to increase the frequency of your sessions by actively looking for ideas that you'd like to communicate.

Therefore, you can ask the universe questions or tell the universe to see something you've never seen before. You could use your third eye to ask the universe to show you your mom when she was ten years old. young. Try to play around with different perspectives using your third eye because you're only limited to your personal perspective within this world. There is a different perspective beyond this one.

In other words suppose that you'd like to go back in time and feel something through your third eye. You might feel what it was like being a baby boy born the world, or as a soldier who drops bombs. Any perspective is open to you. Therefore, you are free to begin exploring this in various ways.

After each session, grab the hands of your partner and gently rub them to get them warm and then put your two hands in close proximity to your third eye region and your eyes like in case you're doing a strenuous exercise. If you're working out hard exercise routine it's best to warm your muscles. Therefore, the method of transferring the heat from your hands to your third eye will aid you in learning to make sense of this new experience as well as the new issues you're asking your brain to think about. You're not limited to the things you can see by looking. Consider this as asking for a way to open up in your body. Sometimes, you won't even require sitting down to open your third eye in order to open it. Occasionally, it will open automatically. This means that you'll leave your work at breathing, working, and looking for information from the extra dimension to enter into the physical dimensions.

The signs of activating your third eye

There will be between sessions a variety of signs that result of activating the third eye. It will be possible to experience clairvoyance, the ability to hear and recent experiences of channeling the third eye, altered patterns of sleep, intense dreaming that is lucid and intense heat. You may also feel electric tingling on your hands, spine neck and head, sudden surges of emotion that are difficult to be able to explain, untreated problems and negative memories extending onto the surface.

The majority of people who are activating their chakras for the third eye will tend to experience extreme food sensitivities. You may be irritated by certain foods or drawn to certain foods that you weren't eating before. You'll experience an increase in the sensitivity that you experience. You'll become more aware of loud sounds and scents and textures that never been a problem for you previously. You'll begin to notice the energy. You may experience symptoms of detox like skin irritations, headaches. This is the result of your increased frequency.

It will be impossible for you to be able to control the toxins stored inside your body. You'll experience sessions of intense inspiration that will force you to be able hold yourself back no matter how hard you attempt. You will experience an incredible level of greater creativity. The events you experience change completely, either positiv or negativ. You'll begin to realize that time is speeding ahead of you realize it. Everyone will be an instructor close to you and it will appear like you are in the middle of a conversation with the universe. speak to you about everything and everybody.

You'll start to see and feel the manifestation of form in them. The numbers will begin repeating themselves and appear for you over and over again. There will be numbers like four four four, one 1, one and five Five five, five.

Mechanical and electrical devices will be able to stop working for you.

Vertigo is a common occurrence or dizziness. You may also experience more nail growth and hair growth, irregular heartbeats. The heart will begin to beat as your heart enters the rhythm of your frequency.

Numerous symptoms throughout your body can be seen as you're opening your third eyes. Every person receives sensory information in a variety of ways. These forms can be emotional, spiritual, physical and mental. This is why there are four main categories: psychics, four.

Mental intuition

The mind-body intuitives are the ones who trigger the third eye most. The ones who can see the clairvoyance of images.

Emotional intuition

The emotional instinct can be described as the kind that can make a huge impact on your mind.

Spiritual intuition

The spiritual sense lets you know what is happening even though you do not be able to pinpoint the exact way you are aware. It will not offer any precise mental or physical images, but it will simply let you know what you are aware of.

Physical intuition

The physical intuition allows you to feel the world around you, which means through actual physical sensations that your body interprets to you.

There is a primary language that is the channel through which psychic information gets to you. Therefore, you will be able to see is that your third eye is a particular sense that is your most powerful cycle sense, will be activated and will expand as you be able to receive more information via it, and eventually the spillover effect will occur.

As the information it gathers from other dimension locations is overloaded, this information can be transferred onto the following faculty. Thus, a naive mental person might see more images once your third eye is open You will then begin to feel the things of other dimensions , too.

We all have the same intuitive meanings we feel to a certain degree the various ways to draw information from the universe of the beyond However, each person has a particular one that is the primary solution.

If you see you as psychic, who is able to perceive information through your emotional senses, this means that you are opening the third eye.

Your emotions will rise and you'll become more emotional. When the emotion reaches its peak then you'll start to perceive images and to experience physical sensations. Thus, opening your third Eye does not just impact the ability of clairvoyance.

You must be prepared to let this occur, even if it's uncomfortable for you; however, firstof all, you need to be able to a point of alignment with what the world is trying to demonstrate.

However, if you notice an increase in resistance and you realize that it's normal and everybody goes through this process at some point So, it's the right time to let it go. You'll be the one to allow the information that is coming to you, so you'll make the choice, and you'll have complete control.

Chapter 9: What Is The Third Eye?

In everyday life there are certain times when you've encountered people with an exceptionally strong and clear sense of. They appear to have a unique intuition for everything.

It's as if they possess an extremely unique sense. Maybe you've observed that your heart or instincts guide you in the right direction . It is also possible that you can see things prior to when they happen. When talking about this natural ability it is also referred to as the third eye.

The eye of the third, sometimes referred to as"the eye of the crown," represents the sixth chakra among our seven major chakras. It is also known as forehead chakra. It is designed to be able to see things clearly. The eye on the forehead can assist in expanding consciousness and is the reason for a very sensitive perception.

Third eye vision is typically depicted as a mark on your forehead. The symbol of the third eye can also be the "Ying-Yang" symbol between the eyebrows or an elevated eye that has long eyelashes and an extreme, warm, and sultry look.

What is the location of the Third Eye? and WHO HAS A FOREHEAD EYE?

The majority of human being has a third-eye since the time of birth. It is located in between your eyes over the nose, and slightly elevated between the eyebrows i.e. it is centered around between the eyebrows. The third eye may be viewed as a link towards the inner soul. The people who are in harmony with their body as well as mind and spirit will also experience an energetic third eye. Contrarily those who live their lives more slack, run the possibility of losing the third eye. But, this isn't as bad since there is always the chance to train and activate the eye's third. We are talking about an opening in the third eye.

A person who thinks about things rationally, and is more led and convinced by the facts, doesn't give the third eye the chance to unlock the doorway to spiritual energy. But, if you make an enduring connection to the center of your energies, also known as the known as ajna, or the third eye could serve as spiritual guidance.

You've probably encountered the phrase: "My gut simply tells me that" This assertion indicates a deep relationship to our souls, a huge awareness and an active third eye.

There are many people who do not have to deal with this issue often think it is a sign of madness or speak of luck an exceptionally good sense. However, it is not the result of luck, but rather of being in harmony and listening to your body. It shows that there are invisible powers that allow us in recognizing and judging"the "whole" beyond the rational mind.

In India Indians are living their lives in complete harmony with their third eye. Through the bindi, which is the area between the eyes the third eye is a symbol that is visible such as it is believed that the Hindu God Shiva can be seen by the third eye. In a world where it is a normal aspect of everyday life, it's naturally easier to handle and be involved by the 3rd eye rather than do it in a culture built on rational thinking.

However, not just in Hinduism as well as in Taoism as well as in Taoism, the Chinese doctrine that Third eye training occurs naturally through meditation.

What do the pineal glands have to relate to the third eye?

The pineal gland can be described as a tiny gland that is located in the middle of the brain. It is sometimes referred to as epiphysis. The gland got its German name due to the fact that its shape recalls a tiny pinecone. The gland is accountable for our mental well-being. This makes it more significant than the insignificant "thing" could suggest. It is accountable for mental, physical and spiritual wellbeing.

The pineal gland is responsible for the internal timer in our body. It regulates our sleep cycle and allows us to live at peace with the subconscious. In the daytime serotonin is released by the brain. It is then converted by is converted by the pineal gland to melatonin during the night. Both are messenger chemicals that are produced by the body, called neurotransmitters.

But, who says we're dealing with an organ present and is not connected to a matter of luck, rather than being in harmony and listening to your body. It is a proof that there are invisible powers that allow us to see and assess what constitutes the "whole" beyond the rational mind.

In India Indians are living their lives in total harmony with their third eye. Through the bindi, which is the area between the eyes the third eye has a visual symbol like it is believed that the Hindu God Shiva has always been represented through an eye third. In a world where it is a normal element of daily routine, it's obviously easier to manage and be involved by the 3rd eye rather than do it in a society built on rational thought.

Not only in Hinduism but also in Taoism as well as in Taoism, the Chinese method that it is believed that the eye of third training can be achieved naturally through meditation.

What is the pineal gland's role to have to do with the third eye?

Pineal glands are a tiny gland that is located in the middle of the brain. It's sometimes referred to as epiphysis. The gland was given its German name due to its shape which is similar to a tiny pinecone. The gland is accountable for our mental well-being. Therefore, it is more significant than the insignificant "thing" could suggest. It is the primary factor in physical well-being, mental well-being and spiritual wellbeing.

The pineal gland regulates your internal rhythm. It regulates our sleep cycle and assists us in living at peace with the subconscious. In the daytime serotonin, the hormone produced by the brain that the pineal gland transforms into melatonin in the night. Both are messenger chemicals created by the body. called neurotransmitters.

But, anyone who claims that we're dealing here with an organ that exists and does not have any connection to third eyes is only correct in a limited sense. Of course the pineal gland is evident in contrast to an eye that is third. It's been proven scientifically that the lifestyle changes cause the pineal gland's size to decrease ever further until it is atrophied. A functioning third eye mindful lifestyle and harmony of the mind, body and spirit also help ensure the pineal gland is not shrink and atrophy. Numerous diseases and their effects such as sleep disorders to Alzheimer's disease, can be avoided to a significant extent by living with a sense of consciousness.

The very possibility of securing yourself from the so-called affluent illnesses will give you an incentive to look the third eye and stimulate it.

Chapter 10: What Are Clairvoyant Capabilities?

A clairvoyant can be described as someone who claims to perceive data that is not a part of the normal abilities through Extrasensory Recognition (ESP) and is believed by others to have these capabilities. It can also be used to represent show-off entertainers who employ techniques like prestidigitation, cold perusing and hot perusing to convey the existence of these abilities. It may also represent information about the psyche that will influence the world in a profound way and also to the supernatural powers believed to be confirmed by such people as, Uri Geller.

The MANY DISTINCT PSYCHIC ABSILITIES

1. Perceptiveness

The well-known mystic capability called hyper vision refers to "clear seeing" and includes seeing things that isn't visible to our eyes. It could be objects, people, creatures or invisible spirits. The people who are affected by these forces may as well "see" events such as the ones that have occurred before or are happening right now, and in the future.

2. Clairaudience

Clairaudience is a reference to "clear hearing" and can refer to hearing voices and sounds which are not perceived by the human hearing. It encompasses hearing voices that are addressed from spirits. It also includes voices in the head, or from creatures or even sounds that come from sleeping objects.

3. Clairsentience

Clairsentience can also be referred to as "clear inclined," which includes the capability to feel vibrations that the five faculties of physicality cannot discern in the real world.

Instantly, you meet someone and you experience the sensation of sadness or fear immediately. It's related to the weather.

4. Clairalience

Clairalience means "clear scent," and incorporates having the possibility of smelling scents that are not recognized by the human nose.

For instance, someone with this trait may out of thin air can smell the odor that a carcass emits in the time of their death, or smell flowers or even consuming motivations when they enter an area, even though there aren't any flowers or motivational figures in the room.

5. Clairgustance

Clairgustance refers to "clear drinking" and also includes tasting something that's not in your mouth.

The model could serve as a blood sample as you drive in the vicinity of a place where someone was being killed.

6. Claircognizance

Claircognizance is also known as "clear understanding" and can refer to quick-thinking or feeling a hunch suddenly.

A model. Having this power gives you moments of focus on people or certain events. A model is a place where someone is in danger or they are being observed in a way that is observable. Each moment this sensation is felt the person's instinct is always correct.

7. Astral Projection

Astral projection is based upon the probability that a person has a soul or a spirit self-destruct away from physical body. The ability is realized through via an out-of-body experience in which the astral body, or soul is able to separate itself from physical body and travels anywhere it desires.

For the major part, occurs at the time of reflection, similar to when your body is asleep.

8. Air Reading

The capacity is based on the possibility that every person has a climate that has their. The quality can be seen in different shades and ranges from 16'-18" away from the body. The term "environment" refers to an electromagnetic field that each living thing is a part of that communicates to a person's personality and destiny, character and soul.

People who are able to read about qualitycan swiftly reveal a person's personality regardless of whether they're luckier or not know.

9. Programmed Writing

The people who possess this ability are able to create written reports that are derived from the deep world, also known as psychography.

The person loses control over their consciousness and allows spirits from a great source to control and write on paper what they intend to convey.

10. Divination

Hyper vision is the technique to ask questions. Through the use of sophisticated devices, the answers are provided and it is one of the types of clairvoyant abilities which can be quickly taught and mastered.

Different types of divinations include the use of gem stones as well as runes, tarot card readings, soul sheets and more.

11. Vitality Healing

This is a type of alternative medicine where the vitality of the healer is transferred to another person, thereby increasing their capacity to repair itself.

It is usually concluded by the healer actually interacting with the patient or hands-off healing in which the healer simply applies his hands to the body of the patient. In the same way the healing of separation should be possible if the healer can think and move in the presence of an individual who isn't actually present.

12. Mediumship or Channeling

Mediumship, also known as Channeling, is one of the most well-known and dangerous forms of mystic powers. It involves using your body as a means to communicate with the vast world. Mediums allow spirits to take the responsibility of their body and be able to share their wisdom to the world.

The main reason people use mediumship is when people who have lost family members and friends require a conversation with the dead to determine the cause of death.

13. Remote Viewing

People who are developing mystic talents will discover that this to be one of the many psychic abilities which can be learned and mastered.

The data accumulated by the clairvoyant is usually not simple and can be found in the form of examples, images, or energies, and then the person who is watching them decodes the information.

14. Precognition

Precognition is the ability to predict the future events to be. It is also the ability to see events in their imaginations or flashes of thoughts. These warnings are typically erratic and wildly difficult to manage.

15. Mystic Surgery

A single of the more disputed mystic abilities, it is refined in the Philippines and also a few pieces of Brazil. The process of clairvoyant medical treatment involves cutting a mystic cut across the body as well as "pulling out" damaged tissues within the body. This is followed with a melody or a plea to the world of the supernatural.

16. Psychometry

Psychometry, also known as psychoscopy is the ability to gather information about spirits when you touch an item that they have recently acquired.

It's based on the idea that people channel their deep energies into objects and then abandon their energies, allowing the mystic to create impressions.

17. Screaming

The ability to receive clairvoyant messages through the use of instruments, such as an expensive stone ball or mirror. This is an art that is typically mastered by seers or soothsayers.

18. Retrocognition

Retrocognition refers to the ability to recognize events that have taken place prior to.

19. Supernatural power

Have you ever been in a film where someone could move objects and not touch them in any way? This type of supernatural force is known as supernatural power. It's the power to change the state of things that are lifeless and, in all probability living things using the force of the mind.

The most common and collective knowledge possessed by those who possess supernatural powers is to turn spoons.

20. Clairvoyance

Clairvoyance is the capacity to read minds, the same as if you were talking to someone else via his brain. It also includes the ability to influence the other person through messages sent via the account.

A portion of clairvoyance also clairvoyant communication with animals that pet mystics "talk" towards animals using channels of vitality that connect spirits, sending them images or messages.

Chapter 11: The Third Eye

Third eye also referred to as the inner eye. It is tiny gland in the endocrine system, which produces a hormone known as Melatonin. This hormone can affect the wellbeing, happiness and modulation of an individual's patterns when they are asleep or awake. It is thought to be an invisble eye that provides the illusion of seeing far beyond the normal view. A lot of people believe that it's a gateway that allows you to access the inner world of consciousness as well as to a world of higher levels of consciousness. The third eye, scientifically called the pineal gland is situated close to the central part in the brain.

For years the purpose of the gland been unexplored. Recently spiritual schools, esoterics and mystical traditions have always recognized and confirmed the functions of the pineal gland. They have always recognized that the pineal gland works as a link between the physical and spiritual realm. Humans are blessed with this type of energy because it is the greatest quality of energy in an extraordinary way. It is in sync with the hypothalamus gland which controls the body's appetite, sexual desire and aging process, among others. Once you awaken your pineal gland one will experience at the base of the brain a sense of pleasure. The pineal gland is a way of the focus of your mind. Focusing helps you trust what you see in your physical world. Once you are able to see your physical world, you'll recognize the distinction between thoughts that are normal and thoughts connected to the third eye.

The science-based explanation of the pineal gland could have was initially an eye, and it gets signals via light as well as our retinas. The concept of"the third eye" is that the "third eye" allows us to perceive what could be and see possibilities beyond the normal eye view.

Every person has access to your third eye. It can happen in situations like when you have strong feelings regarding something and then acts upon it.

When your eye isn't active you are unable to think on their own, since they're extremely unflexible in thinking. If your third eye is hyper-active it is likely that you live in a realm of over-the-top fantasies and excessive hallucinations.

To fully comprehend your third eye it is necessary to be aware that it's an indication of an elevated state of mind where you is able to perceive the world in an ethereal way. It's not about having psychic abilities or supernatural powers, it's nevertheless, the ability to be more in control of your mind and feelings. Within Hinduism and Buddhism the word "eye" is used as a symbol of enlightenment, and is known as the eye of wisdom.

The function of the third eye.

A few of the functions associated with the 3rd eye comprise of concentration imagination, visualization, recall of dreams as well as clairvoyance, perception understanding, intelligence etc. Here are the tasks it performs based on its flexibility:

It regulates the flow of thoughts and mental images going through the mind. All thoughts and messages, good or not will be replayed by the pineal gland.

The third eye can help to read, comprehend and communicate using your mind. It allows you to influence or control actions and thoughts of others. When you have interactions with other people their thoughts and opinions can affect you either in a positive or negative ways.

It is a director and synthesizer for energy or force.

The third eye connects the physical world to the spiritual realm. It allows you to transcend your imagination into another dimension of spirituality.

The gland of the pineal gland produces hormones, such as melatonin. It acts as an antioxidant and aids in combating free radicals which damage cells.

Melatonin, the hormone located inside the pineal gland regulates your sleep as well as you wake-up cycle.

Melatonin aids to prevent disease and other health issues such as anxiety, insomnia and fatigue. Melatonin is able to do this by defending your white blood cells from radiation-induced damage.

The pineal glands are also associated to our reproductive system in a manner that when the pineal gland gets damaged, sexual organs expand faster.

Chapter 12: Open Your Third Eye Through Meditation

"When you have your head at peace as well as your 3rd eye open, you are able to discern and understand what is happening many thousands of miles from your location."

- FREDERICK LENZ

Invoking the Third Eye

Relax. Let's begin by counting backwards starting from one hundred until zero. You can count with your mind or in loud voice whatever you prefer, it isn't a problem. Once you've finished your count, you'll have to be prepared to open your third eye. Concentrate your attention to your forehead which is that your third eye is supposed to be. You will notice that everything is dim, except for the third eye's chakra. When your third eye chakra is finally active, your mind will be peaceful, but functioning at a different level. The brain's two sides are working in tandem and consequently you'll be aware of the energy that is within your.

It is important to recognize that you have been using the third eye when your body is experiencing an increase in energy flowing through it and surrounding it.

You will also be able to determine whether your third eye is activated by being focused on a single object or image and your brain is completely absorbed by it. It will be as if there is no other thing in the world except the image or object will appear as when you're in a state of state of trance.

Experience the Third Eye

Different people respond differently to activation by the eye's third. It's not uncommon to see your mind flashing different visual effects like pictures from nature, waterfalls trains, people as well as other scenes you have observed previously. Some people refer to it as the ability to look at your thoughts similar to projected on a film screen that is in front of your eyes.

Focus upon your 3rd eye about 10 minutes. It's normal to feel headaches when you first attempt to open your third eye. Be assured that as you progress, your headaches will diminish gradually. To get you to train that third eye for your primary eye, focus your attention only on one specific image. It could be a number, or it could be an object, just try to keep your attention on the image you've selected. The more you focus on the third eye and the more you will naturally will begin using it in unintended ways.

Take a look at a practice of Hatha Yoga

The third eye is a part of the mind. Meditation is part of the more thorough exercise in Hatha Yoga, which usually incorporates physical exercises as well as relaxation and strength training. The chakras, also known as the energy centers in our body are usually connected, and in order to achieve third eye chakra it is necessary to first traverse the chakras below. The Ajna chakra - also known as the third eye chakra is the highest chakra on the body, located just beneath the crown chakra. In order to activate, not just the chakra of third eye but all of them it is necessary to engage in an exercise like Hatha Yoga, where you apply your body to specific postures, not just by meditative. We'll discuss more about the chakras in the following chapter.

Figure 11: Do yoga to open your chakras.

Chapter 13: Identifying Your Third Eye's Nature

It's almost impossible for anyone to master all the abilities of the third eye over the course of their life. There are numerous skills that can be acquired however, it takes lots of work to be able to master these abilities. These skills are usually referred to as third eye-like abilities. All the possibilities are there due to your connection with your third eye as well as the possibilities you can accomplish using it.

The function of a person's third eye is similar to language. The process of learning a new language may take a long time to learn regardless of years of training. It's the same with Third Eye. Also, it is possible to learn a variety of languages. As with language, the more you study, the more easy it becomes to master since you'll be able to spot patterns and utilize this information to improve your understanding.

Certain people are only looking to open their third eye to gain greater insight however, they might not master the art but are content with enjoying the majority of the benefits described in the chapter on the second. Some will refine their skills and gain the ability to astral project or look the future. A select group of people, they will learn about different natures over their lives.

The Natures in the third Eye

What's the first image that pops up in your head when you hear psychic ability? Does it bring up images of women in Bangles and scarves looking at a crystal ball or drawing lines on the palm of a hand? They're all Hollywood-style images. There aren't any typical characteristics which a person with these abilities has in common. Anyone can benefit from the power that the eye has and bring supernatural abilities to their daily lives. While the information below isn't exhaustive but it can give you an some idea of the capabilities that those who develop their abilities are able to achieve after opening the third eye.

Clairsentience

Clairsentience can sense spirits and energies that are past, present or even future. It can be as simple as being able to see the past lives of someone else or having a conversation with someone and learning crucial details about their lives upon touching them. Auras and energies can play a role however, it is typically resulted from channeling the energy of someone upon physical contact.

Astral Projection

Aspect projection is the projection of your consciousness outside your body. It could lead you to another location in the world or in a different moment, or even to a different level. In most cases, astral projection can be in comparison to an out-of-body experience. The primary distinction is that astral projection happens because you choose to do, while the experience of being out-of-body happens involuntary. When you are astral projected, you won't be restricted to the exact physical limitations like your physical body. You are able to move through walls and through doors.

Clairvoyance

This is one of the most commonly used psychic abilities. It is the ability to perceive visions, auras or spirits, and also being able to see into the future or past. That is, of course, the psychic ability typically depicted in Hollywood as clairvoyants spiritual mediums, and other kinds of fortune-tellers.

Telekinesis

Telekinesis's power is extremely rare. It is a Hollywood popular film, where it is shown as a superpower in films like 'X-Men' , or as a force in the film 'Star Wars'. Telekinesis is basically the ability to move objects that are within your head using your brain.

Claircognizance

The ability of claircognizance can also be called 'clear knowledge'. It refers to the capacity to recognize something without prior studies or knowledge of the matter. It is often believed to be handed down to an individual through their higher self or an angelic guide.

Mediumship

The people who are able to open their third eye and are able to speak directly to spirits have developed the skill of mediumship, which is also known as psychic channeling. It is not unusual for mediums to cooperate with psychics or acquire additional psychic capabilities. In some instances the medium talks to Spirit and then listens and gathers data this way. Some mediums permit spirits to take over their body and speak directly through the medium's voice.

Clairaudience

The ability to hear sounds beyond what is thought to be normal human perception. The majority of these sounds originate from a different dimension or the realm of the spiritual. The sounds of voices can be heard but noises and music often cross paths. Sometimes, those who have clairaudience may be able to receive messages linked to specific inanimate objects like artifacts, crystals and minerals.

Precognition

Precognition refers to the ability to discern the future and anticipate future things.

Precognition occurs in various ways, and sometimes it is an outcome of extra-sensory perception (ESP) or the ability to see. In other instances, those who are precognitive learn about the future via detailed dreams.

Psychometry

Psychometry is the process of activating information through physical contact with the object or going to an area. It can be used to discover what has happened in a specific location, to help locate the person or thing that's lost, or uncover other details. A few people have developed their third eye so that they are able to use this similar ability in order to talk with other animals through the detection of emotions and images that come from the animal's brain.

Automatic Writing

Automatic writing happens when one connects to the other side. It's a method of communicating with spirits that have gone on to other planes or are trapped in different planes. The conscious mind is not present when writing automatically. It's like you're in a state of trance. Your hands will glide effortlessly across the paper.

Retrocognition

Certain people see only into the past, but not to the present. Retrocognition is typically acquired through dreams, where you can see events from the past that you were involved in, your past lives, or even other individuals.

Clairgustance

Have you ever had the chance to taste something you remember vividly, perhaps the favorite dessert your mother used to create or the homemade spaghetti sauce your father made? People with the gift of clairgustance can taste things without actually touching them.

Divination

Divination is the art of using tools to collect evidence or data from the spiritual realm and then employing techniques to interpret it into our physical reality. It is possible for people to use this to discover certain things, gain insight into the present, discover the past, or even predict the future.

Divination is based on the concept that the ethereal universe as well as the world of physical are in the same connection. The objects or tokens are used to gather information provide clues spiritual energy, or a means of communication. A few of the most well-known translations are made up such as crystal balls, tea leaves pendulums, tarot cards the scrying process, Ouija boards, and the bibliomancy to mention some.

Telepathy

The ability of telepathy allows you to discern the thoughts of other people as well as their mood or future. It is an personal connection to the mind. Some individuals develop to the point of the ability to alter or even create thoughts into the minds of others. This is a possibility to communicate with humans, but people who have developed this technique can also communicate with animals.

The psyche Empathy

Certain individuals are more sensitive than others due to an increased emotional intelligence. The term "psychic empathy" refers to an identical phenomenon in which you can feel or sense other people's emotions. This is often done by detecting the aura or energy field of a person instead of focusing on physical cues like an individual who is naturally compassionate could.

Etheric Sight

Certain people are able to perceive things that aren't physically touched such as books or letters. While this is akin to vision

X-rays, it's far from being able to untie someone's eyes. Instead, etheric vision allows people to be able to see through solids as well as into solids.

Identifying the nature of your Third Eye

Many people agree with the importance of setting goals in life, in order to assist to get to a certain perfect point. This helps them stay focused and helps them stay on the right course. Just as you set the goal by setting a goal, you can set the goals to your 3rd eye through determining the nature of your eyes.

The third eye opening is an action. Some people are able to experience their abilities in a natural way, while others discover that their talents are hidden in the depths of. A lot of people spend the majority of their lives developing their third eye, educating it to function according to the way they wish to.

It is a given that an inherent natural against. nurture argument is in the picture in this instance. Certain people are more predisposed to particular abilities more than others. This could have something to be related to the way you've used your third eye in your life , or if your soul has been previously linked to your third eye. In certain Buddhists faiths there is a belief that the soul lives in the same place time and repeatedly until you achieve awakening. This is the concept of Reincarnation.

The best method to discover the character that your eye has isn't to push it. Set aside time for relaxation and meditation throughout your day. Be aware that , the harder you attempt to force your third eye to perform a task the less likely that the behavior you want to force to happen. One way you can improve your abilities is to practice regular meditation on the third eye. It is possible to connect with someone who is trained in your particular area should you wish however, this doesn't necessarily guarantee that you'll achieve the type of personality you want to attain.

The nature of the Third Eye and Mantras

If you're looking to concentrate on your eye's third in a manner that will help you gain the ability to do something using mantras, you can do this to help you fall into a state of calm and to open your third eye. Mantras help you set the intention of a specific goal, while not affecting the focus. They aid in the process of meditation and relax, instead of demanding greater concentration.

If you are going to utilize a mantra to open your third eye, it is crucial to select a mantra with an intention that is in line with your goal. For instance, you're not likely to envision the future if you're using a mantra that makes an association to other realms.

Be sure you continue practicing once you've developed your skills. While most people will only acquire one third eye nature during their lifetime However, many of the techniques are in close relation. Similar to the languages, you'll notice that as you recognize patterns and know how to direct your attention understanding the various natures gets more simple.

Chapter 14: Transformation Of The Personal The Third Eye Chakra

Ajna chakra awakening can open up new geographic regions of potential and beauty. We discover that we're much more than we thought and maybe even more than we imagined that we would be. We view our reflections from a clean perspective and find ourselves in a heightened state of consciousness in which we are able to see how we're affected and inflicted pain by the other human beings in the world, their places, and the styles all around us. This is an inner instead of an external change. (An observer looking us may look at no difference.) Instead of being trapped in a sea of words and worries, we have the opportunity to bring more joy and grace in our lives as a result of beginning the eye chakra at 1/3.

Pineal-Gland-Banner-Ver-1.Zero

In the ever-present dance of duality encountered in our everyday lives, there's the chance of being out of line in the maze of potential limitations to achieving tranquility. Concentrating our minds on the bright side of the 1/three eye chakra is much less difficult in the same way that we can certainly accept an inner balance of awareness of the world. "Ajna chakra acts as the center of witnessing where one becomes an indifferent observer of all sports as well as those within the body and mind," writes Swami Sivananda Saraswati. "When Ajna chakra is awakened it means that meaning of symbols is reflected into awareness, and intuitive memories are created and one can become an observer."

"Witness focus means looking at something at something without being affected, and without judgment," provides Swami Muktananda. "Say in a particular example, two human beings arguing, and one of them is watching. The person who is looking, and is not worried and will be the Witness. The indwelling witness watches all activities of the daytime world without focusing on the events." Certain teachers apply witness recognition while watching a film. You are seated in the theatre and are completely focused on the action happening on the screen before you, but you do not more engage in the movie. It's a great option, however like numerous 1/3 eye/ajna chakra abilities it could also be triggered in a polarity spectrum from small amounts of. (Check for tension on your feet during an undetermined time in the future of a terrifying scene. If your feet are twitching or curling it's because you're within the area of goals and emotions.) In the midst of a large-scale recognition of witnesses Self is unaffected and genuinely watching. In the absence of that it is possible to feel your toes are squeezing.

Chapter 15: Diet Changes For A Healthy Pineal Gland

As we've discussed in previous chapters, the substances which are present in our foods or water supply can exacerbate the issue of the third eye becoming blocked or a pineal gland that has been calcified. Removal of foreign chemicals or excess minerals is an excellent method to restore the pineal gland and stop it from getting blocked again.

To cleanse the pineal gland There are a range of foods which can accelerate the process. It is important to consume food items that attract the calcified substance and dissolve it order to flush them out of your pineal gland.

In general, food items with antioxidant properties could help in this regard. Vitamins E and C are naturally antioxidants, and should be consumed regularly to remove contaminants from the pineal gland. They also assist in eliminating free radicals, which are particles that cause damage to cells, from the body, thereby slowing down the process of aging.

Vitamin C is present in large amounts in citrus fruits, as well as dark greens that are leafy. Vitamin E can be found in a variety of plants, such as aloe along with seeds, nuts and meat. Both kinds of antioxidants can help to boost immunity. A diet that is rich in antioxidants is the most effective source however supplements are readily available.

It is the most natural fluid that lubricates and is believed to be the most universal solvent. It is extremely difficult for the body to flush out toxins if there is no fluid available to aid in their elimination. Water is the major element in urine and when it travels through the kidneys and the bladder system, it absorbs the waste and flushes it out of the body. This is an essential process to ensure that your body is in good state of health.

Cells that have become encased by calcified materials can be cleaned by drinking water. The most common advice is to drink at least half the weight of your body in ounces each day however any improvement in fluid levels could aid in decalcification.

Remember that water from cities almost always contains chlorine and fluoride to treat it, and drinking more fluoride could be detrimental to your health. Although the fluoride is intended to help prevent deficiencies, studies have shown that too much fluoride in city drinking water actually reduces the IQ of children. This can't be beneficial for us! 9: Drink the water in bottles from a safe water source, well water or use a home water filtration system that includes the fluoride filter.

If adding a specific food item to your diet sounds to be a feasible option There are

specific food items that are ric
antioxidants and vitamins and
that could help improve your health and
well-being.

Chlorella is a form of wheatgrass which is a rich source of minerals, vitamins, and antioxidants. It has been proven to rid organs of heavy metals as well as boost the immunity system and helps remove accumulation of calcified matter.

Iodine is a natural mineral that plays a vital role in the various processes in the body. It is required in small amounts to support all organs of the body. It is also able to remove fluoride from your body. Fluoride and iodine are closely related in molecular structure. When cells recognize its iodine structure it immediately absorbs it.

Since they are similar in appearance as well, fluoride and iodine fight to use the exact pathways to cells. If you have higher levels of Iodine in your system it permits less fluoride to be able to bind with cells.

151

This slows down the process of calcification. Instead, fluoride bonds to calcium, and is able to be eliminated from the body.

Iodine is naturally found in dark greens, such as broccoli and spinach as well as seafood and fish. Table salts are usually enhanced with iodine. It was developed decades ago to help fight thyroid problems caused by a lack of the mineral iodine.

Vinegar, especially varieties of apple cider are ideal to decalcify. The acidic properties of vinegar and the bitter taste are essential in removing harmful substances. A small amount of vinegar made from apples can help remove kidney stones. They also ease the symptoms associated with gout reduce blood pressure and lower the levels of blood sugar.

Mix two or three tablespoons with tap water and drink regularly. Don't drink it straight . Rinse the mouth following drinking, as malic acid can damage tooth enamel.

In addition there is evidence to suggest that the consumption of a diet high in alkaline which is the reverse of acid, could be beneficial too. The foods that are alkaline-based are mostly plants and don't require more energy to digest like foods that cause acid when they are absorbed. Proteins and meats contain a lot of nitrogen, and this causes an acidic imbalance within the blood. Although the body is able to regulate this acid with the base of the kidneys, it can cause additional strain to the body's system.

The immune system in general helps in the process of decalcification. A good supply of natural antioxidants and antimicrobials can help keep your body free from the toxins as well as viruses the body needs to contend with. If you're well-nourished, your immune system will focus on removing calcification instead of fighting bacteria.

Natural antimicrobial food sources include garlic, oregano, and onions. Their pungent flavor helps eliminate bacteria. They are frequently supplemented in the flu and cold season to help prevent illnesses and reduce the time of onset. Another interesting supplement for this is the Chaga mushroom , which is native of China in China and Japan. It has been long hailed as having powerful health benefits that include immune-boosting properties in hormone regulation, in addition to antiviral and antitumor properties. It's full of phytochemicals and usually made into tea.

Flavonoids are a component of many foods that can reduce blood pressure and improve blood flow. When blood flow is improved as well as circulation within the pineal gland increases. A steady flow of blood indicates that toxins and minerals do not be calcified as quickly, which allows the pineal gland to release melatonin whenever it wants. Consuming chocolate that is rich (not the milk-based chocolate!) and deep purple and blue fruits such as blueberries or concord grapes may help in this process.

Beets are the next item to be added. Their dark red color is an indication of boron, a different mineral. This assists in removing heavy metals, and also balance calcium intake when it's excessive. It also provides a large source of B vitamins, which are crucial to the overall production of energy.

These foods will certainly help to cleanse the system and reduce the likelihood of building up. It is vital to keep in mind that these foods won't have any effect unless you make an effort to stay clear of food items that helped to calcify this gland in the initial place. They aren't an alternative to clean eating and healthy choices in food.

Making changes to the overall diet by avoiding processed food items and focusing on whole food items in their natural form is a fantastic method to begin a the diet. Replace your grocery store snacks fast food, and similar items with whole food composed of natural ingredients. Remove foods that are high in phosphorus, such as soda, which can cause the process of calcification.

Switch your fast food burger in exchange for a nutritious salad made of beans or chicken. You will not only be receiving more antioxidants, but you'll also be avoiding foods that can contribute to the process of calcification. Healthy eating makes your body perform more efficiently and provides you with more energy. In addition, the low-calorie and salt-free options will prevent you from storing water and adding weight.

To alter your diet, opt for food items that are grown naturally. Fresh vegetables and fruits paired with meat raised responsibly or vegetarian meats are as healthy as they get. Go for whole grains instead of refined grains, and make the all of your meals from plants. Include fruits and vegetables in your food and snack time.

While it is true that fish can lower cholesterol levels However, it is also filled with mercury. Consume these foods in moderation, and make sure to purchase from a reputable source.

Also, avoid substances that are not compatible with the body, like alcohol and caffeine. Cut down or eliminate your consumption of these items for most optimal outcomes. While you're there, refrain from smoking and excessive sugar.

Chapter 16: Sixth Sense

While we're conscious of five sensory experiences common for humans (sight and smell, taste as well as hearing) Many don't fully grasp what the sixth sense actually entails.

Have you seen someone who seems to be aware of what is going to take place before it happens? Do you have a feeling that they're supposed to be doing something, only to find out to be right? It's what is known as the sixth sense. a mechanism that a person's body can detect something which the other five senses can't.

Telepathy is a kind of sixth sense. This means that one can communicate their thoughts with another person or maybe read the thoughts of another, but isn't in of. Comics make fun of this just as real people who have the ability to are able to perform in front of crowds. Similar to other aspects related to the topic, it's extremely controversial, with both believers and those who are not standing their positions.

It is believed that ESP (Extrasensory Perception) has enabled people with ESP to make amazing yet true statements. For example the fire that raged in Sweden in 1759 which Emmanuel Swedenborg proclaimed was occurring close to his home, 300 miles away from where the party he attended.

The sense of sixth has been intensively investigated by scientists for decades and years. There was a time when it was believed at the time that ESP was more powerful when people were relaxed or sleeping. The sleep lab had a subject sleeping in one area while in another room a volunteer was looking at a photograph. There were many people who reported having dreams in which the image was being viewed in the opposite room.

Another type of sixth sense is seen through Out of Body Experiences (OBE). When someone experiences an experience that is near death or even die for a brief period of time before returning in some way, they may be able to describe what's called an experience outside of the body. There are other kinds of OBE's, including the astral projection or travel. Some are unintentional experiences, like dreams of death or near-death, and other types can be induced by meditation or chemical. These OBE's can be linked to third-eye perception because these experiences are associated with a different realm of existence, which the third eye also permits us to experience.

There is a theory that, the moment one sense is absent and the other senses are stronger, they are strengthened. This is evident by a person who is blind and has an acute sense of hearing , for instance. The sixth sense may be included in this idea. Charles Honorton in the 1970's was the first to test this idea, and it remains an active theory. Honorton utilized a test devised by Wolfgang Metzger, dubbed the ganzfeld test. The test utilizes sensory deprivation to reveal the ESP of the person being tested. The results of this test have been the focus of a lengthy and heated debate about whether or not they're random, or if they are conclusive evidence.

The main part in the New Age of thinking involves the Law of Attraction. It is the belief that similar thinking can produce like actions. For instance, if you sit in meditation and imagine yourself getting rich and focus on the thought for long enough, you'll appear "attracted" or will end up within your daily life. Theoretically , this could be utilized together with opening the third eye to focus your attention on these things into a different realm of existence. It is also possible to use your law of attraction aid in opening your third eye. Through visualizing yourself awakening the eye, it could get you in touch to your eye's third quicker.

To help you succeed applying to benefit from the Law of Attraction it is essential to rid you of doubts that you have regarding the goal you're setting. In the same way as in the previous example If you imagine yourself as wealthy but you are unsure that is lingering in your head that says you don't have the right to be so wealthy If you're blocking yourself from starting. To have success, you should utilize meditation to clear these negative thoughts from your head.

Chapter 17: What You Can Do To Maintain Your Third Eye Energized

After you've gone through lots of effort to activate the third eye, and you're having fun with your new lifestyle and you are not looking to allow this eye to deactivate or become inactive. You are aware it is a part of every person, it was already there in you however, you didn't recognize it until you began to look for how to activate the third eye. If you are not able to recognize and acknowledge your eye's third and maximum usage of it a regular basis, you might find yourself wanting to go back to this guide and complete the procedure of activating your 3rd eye.

Things that could deactivate your Third Eye

To ensure that your third eye stays active at all times and you continue to reap the benefits from it, you have to first determine what could deactivate your third eye. When you are aware of the things that can cause this, it is essential to stay away from them. This is your only chance to ensure that your third eye active constantly.

Lifestyle changes must do much for keeping your mind active throughout the day. If you experience sudden changes to your life, you might notice a decline in the spiritual power of your. Since your pineal glands can be closely associated with the powers of your third eye Any changes or negative consequences to your pineal glands may reduce the capabilities or powers from your third eye. Here are a few changes in your lifestyle that could damage the pineal glands.

Excessive hormones are absorbed in processed foods

In excess, artificial sweeteners are consumed

The consumption of toxins in the food we consume today

In excess intake of fluoride, whether it is in the form of toothpaste with fluoride or in drinking water

In excess, sugar consumption or sweets

Toxins that are absorbed from the environment

Consumption of additives in the processed products

These are just some aspects of lifestyle modifications that could have a negative effect on the pineal glands. As the result, you could be unable to keep your third eye active constantly.

Regular Meditation Sessions

In addition to avoiding these issues In addition, be sure to do regular meditation to aid you in getting into the higher realms of your unconscious. The energy is flowing throughout your body. You are connected with the the spiritual universe every moment of the day.

It is also important to be aware of negative thoughts and negative thinking and stay away from all the negative influences that exist within our culture. You must select your friends with care and remain always in a positive mindset every day. These factors will help keep your soul pure and clean, and will help maintain your eye active throughout the day.

Risks you may face once Your Third Eye is Deactivated

After you've figured out what you must accomplish and what things you should avoid You should also be aware of the possible consequences you might be facing if your third eye is shut or deactivated. It can be detrimental physically emotionally, as well as spiritually. If you've lived with your third eye being activated for a long time it is possible that you are not in a position to deal with the effects that could be faced after your third eye is shut.

Following are some of the consequences/situations, you may face if your third eye gets deactivated or closed.

you could experience sleep problems patterns.

You may be ever cautious

You may experience mood shifts

you may find yourself being jealous

You may have trouble with coordination.

your digestive system, sexual system and nervous system may get disturbed

You could get lost throughout your life.

You may discover that your current life is full of uncertainty

You may be negative

You may be one-sided in your perspective

The Pineal Glands Need to be cleansed

The positive side is that it is possible to cleanse your pineal gland, and keep your third eye in perfect condition even if you've deliberately or accidentally damaged it. There are numerous organic extracts and natural products to include as part of your diet to cleanse your pineal gland , and keep it activated or stimulated. A few of these natural components or extracts include:

Ginseng

Zeolite

Blue-green algae

Chlorella

Chlorophyll

Iodine

Hemp seeds

Water melons

Borax

Raw Cacao

Blue skate liver oil

Seaweed

Chapter 18 The Phases Of The Moon

The moon's phases are essential for the practice of magick. Wiccans consider that moonlight has magical properties, and its different phases could result in different outcomes. Therefore, it is crucial to plan your work in accordance to the moon's phases.

The Waxing Moon

It changes from dark to fully-filled and typically takes 14 days to complete the cycle. In several Wiccan rituals positive magick is performed during the time when you see the moon waxing. They seek to attract positive energy and make themselves better. At this point you are able to do rituals to improve your love, money, career and objects.

Waxing Crescent Moon or Crescent Moon

It is often referred to also as the Moon of Regeneration, and is anywhere from 45 to

90@ in advance of sun. In this period, you can plan to gather information, build the foundation or begin to change your life. Also, you can prepare for your future goals. The crescent or waxing moon indicates the best moment to regenerate. At this time, strengthening your body and strengthening it are the most effective since you can absorb both positive and negative energy more efficiently.

1st Quarter (or Waxing Moon

It is also called also known as the Moon of Caution, and can be found between 90 and 135@ in front of the sun. It lasts between 7 and 10 1/2 days following it is the full moon. At this time it is there is a celebration called the Time of Warrior Maiden is commemorated. It is symbolized in the form of Artemis, Minerva, Athena, Diana, and Bridget. It is the ideal moment to develop intuition, instinct and inspiration. Also, it is the ideal time to experience regeneration and renewal.

Waxing Gibbous Moon

It is often referred to by the name of Moon of Endings, and is 135 up to 180@ in front of the sun. At this time over half the moon's surface is illuminated by the sun. This is the best moment to tie up loose ends and get ready for the energy that will come from the full moon.

The Full Moon

It is often referred to by the name of Moon of Celebration and is 180to 255 degrees in front of the sun. At this moment, the entire face that the moon faces is clearly visible. Wiccans are known to use spells only during the time when moonlight is fully full since they believe it is the most potent. They typically do their rituals for three days, which includes the day prior and the day following. Certain groups may even insist that their members work on the various phases of the moon.

A full moon can be the suitable moment to use spells to help spiritual and personal development. It's also a great time for carrying out any significant work. It is possible to cast healing spells and spells to developing your magical skills and sensitivity. Additionally, you can perform spells that will bring you more connected to divinities. Furthermore, you could take part in your own Esbat ritual.

The New Moon

It is often referred to for being the Dark Moon as well as the Moon of Rest and Beginnings. At this time it's right within the solar system and earth, which is the reason it's not visible. This is the only time the solar eclipse can be observed. The moon is located between from 0 to 45° over the sun.

At the time of the the new moon, you are able to make spells to bring new beginnings and ventures. This is the ideal time to take a break, discover new love, gain strength in gratitude and reenergize. It's also the perfect time to let go of unproductive habits. Furthermore, it's the ideal time to start new initiatives.

The time of the new moon is the time when you see the fruits of your hard work. It can also be difficult to conduct work during this time since the moon is not visible. A lot of Wiccans believe that the new moon as a time of fallow, during which they take a break and recharge before performing more intensive activities. Others Wiccans are, however, inclined to view the new moon an opportunity to do magick associated with achieving wish fulfillment.

The Waning Moon

It changes from dark to full and remains that way for several weeks. In this period it is a symbol of God as a Crone and is thus the most suitable to use for divination and deep intuition. Wiccans typically perform a shamanistic ritual when the moon is in waning. They are aiming to eradicate or destroy and then throw away everything they don't want anymore.

The moon's waning phase is the best moment to cast spells to eliminating bad behaviors such as ending a relationship or getting rid of an employment position, or for reducing the burden of debt and other negative aspects. It's also the ideal time to leave and safeguard yourself from people and influencers who are negative to you.

Waning Gibbous or disseminating Moon

It is often referred to by the name of Moon of Retribution or the Moon of the Earth Mothers which is located approximately 225 to 270° over the solar system. At this time it is the best time to review the actions taken, rectify mistakes, resolve disputes and amend any mistakes. Wiccans believe that the moon's waxing phase is connected to everyday issues. They also believe it triggers growth instinctually.

Final Quarter of Waning or Last Quart
Moon Moon

It is sometimes referred to by the name of
Moon of Harvest, and is between 270 and
315@ before the Sun. It is ideal to release
negativity and ending behaviors and
relationships. In this period you should
eliminate anything that creates
obstruction. This is the ideal opportunity
to take a break, relax in recovery, recover,
and prepare yourself to release the energy
released from the moon's new phase.

Chapter 19: The Psychic Abilities Chapter

How to Become a Medium Medium

If you are looking to maintain your eyes on the ball and increase your skills, you should adhere to the advice given in the previous chapters. Make sure you know the things you're being exposed to and how you can do it correctly. Get grounded. Use crystals, oils, meditation, chanting, yoga, etc. Find a teacher who can guide you and guide you. It's important to be able to switch it off and on should you want to use it. If you want to enhance these abilities more, we have a few ways to practice.

Ten Strategies to Enhance Your abilities to communicate

It is best to commit to doing every day a single activity. Do it until it feels natural and comfortable Then add another activity and do the same.

Meditate

When you practice meditation daily you are connecting with the universe and increasing your frequency and awareness. It is important to raise your vibration to match that of the spiritual world that exists at a high frequency. You should meditate for 10 to 15 minutes each day to begin. You can increase the time by five minutes as often as you can.

Psychometry

It is the process of analyzing the energy levels of objects. Try it by using something (something that has a long history, or metal could hold lots in energy). Relax and collect impressions so that you can see or hear things about the history. It is also possible to contemplate the past.

Clairvoyance-Flowers

This exercise will allow you to develop the ability to see with clairvoyance using the flower visualization. By placing fresh flowers before your eyes, you can simply observe them for a couple of minutes and then shut your eyes. While your eyes are closed, imagine every flower in your head to create the picture. If you can gather any thoughts from this, it's more than enough! Create mental images as you proceed.

Clairvoyance- Random

Similar to the earlier activity but with more randomness. Relax and concentrate your mind on the area of your third eye. Do not think about it and let your mind create images in your eye's lens. Let them appear and go and note the way they appear.

Antique Stores

These are wonderful locations to visit since they are rich in history that involve people and places that will be revealed to you once you have developed your ability to become into their rhythm. The antiques also emit their own sound vibrations. Be aware of the sensations you perceive or observe as you go through this. Make this a habit whenever you are in a position to go to a temple and try as many times as you can, paying close attention to the way your senses are developed.

6. Symbol Books

Our senses frequently detect symbols that later need to be understood, and they don't always have the same significance. When you are developing your abilities , it's an excellent idea to be aware of the various symbols you'll interact with. Try this out in solitude. in a peaceful space or in a meditative state, ask the spirit to show you signs to represent things you're thinking about and write them down in a notebook you've got to this end. They may pop on your mind in the near future and they could be an element of your interpretational vocabulary.

7. Clairaudience

To improve your hearing ability. Pay greater attention and more attentive to everyday sounds around you to expand your awareness. You'll learn to be aware of sounds since you're picking the sounds that are around you after the third eye of your brain is arousing.

8. Family Pictures

Find old family photos. Find as long as you could. Make use of your senses to perceive things through the intensity of the photograph that you are able to. Take note of them too. Do this with different photos and extend to those you might not have met to get impressions.

9. JOURNAL

Request guidance for the issue that could cause a problem in your daily life. Record the thoughts that occur to your mind. The senses could manifest in various shapes that you need to discern, which can add another layer to capturing the experience in writing. It is also recommended to keep your dream journal and make use of it right away (no longer than 10 seconds after awakening!) for the purpose of being able to recall the numerous dreams you probably had during the night.

10. VIBRATIONAL FOODS

Healthy, whole, and organic, high-vibration food items is not just better for your overall well-being, but also for your mental health too. Like what was mentioned about meditation and increasing your frequency, you can make use of food items to boost your vibration. If you consume poor food, it can lower your vibration. You require higher vibrations of energy to function in higher dimensions.

Research thoroughly. Foods that are living, particularly raw and organic foods , as well as organic produce , are free from things like radiation, growth in farms, wastewater and other polluted waters as well as pesticides such as larvicides, fungicides and so on.

A unique form of photography that was created by Russia along with Eastern Europe called Kirlian photography has proven that our food products are able to emit glowing colors! These are vital life force or energy that emanates through the food. Organic and raw foods have the highest energy fields. Examples include raw slices of orange or broccoli. These are more energetic than cooked or "dead" foods like cut-up steaks or broccoli that have been cooked are the ones with the least energy fields. Even raw fish in comparison to cooked fish has demonstrated a greater energy field.

Avoid processed food as well as artificial foods disguised as food (but they aren't) as well as foods that contain added chemicals. It is also recommended to avoid stimulants, including caffeine. Alcohol is a nerve system stimulant and a depressant of the nervous system. The latter function can cause agitation in the body. It can also be harmful to the body as well as the mind. The meat you consume must remain as clean as is possible. If you eat foods that stimulate your body then you are the food you eat, which is full of vibratory forces.

To aid in the awakening of your third eye and growth, you need to be as proactive as you can to raise and sustain your energy. Humans living in this world of three dimensions face challenges, but we can adapt and increase the vibrational energy through our daily habits, yoga, meditation, and other forms of exercise, by positive thinking, and other techniques that are discussed in this book.

Conclusion

After you have a better understanding of exactly what Third Eye is, you are able to begin using it every throughout the day. Begin by making sure that it's accessible in the first place. Follow the steps that are easy to follow in this book and see your life transform in a positive direction. With a greater awareness of your own life and the people around you, you can feel more confident in working on specific projects and interacting with other people. This is due to the intuitive ability of your third eye will be able to alert you that certain movements could cause danger to you and also when other moves could be beneficial. If you are able to do exercises to open and close the third eye you need to be sure that you're taking full control over your life, which is a pleasant feeling and a beneficial practice for practical purposes.

CPSIA information can be obtained
at www.ICGtesting.com
Printed in the USA
LVHW020238290423
745602LV00004B/548